Cooking at the Café
Lunch and Dinner Fare

Francie in her kitchen

The Café Crew

Cooking at the Café
Lunch and Dinner Fare

recipes from
Café Croissant
215 SW 5th Street
Corvallis • Oregon

by

Francie O'Shea

Design, handlettering, and simple illustrations by
Francie O'Shea

Cover and chapter illustrations by
Lynn Humme

Copyright © 1992 by Francie O'Shea

All rights reserved. No portion of this book may be reproduced in any form without written permission from the author.

To obtain additional copies of this book, use the order forms on the last page or write:

    Cooking at the Café
    2910 N.W. Hayes
    Corvallis, OR 97330

Suggested retail price is $14.95 plus $3.25 in shipping charges.

Third Printing

ISBN 0-9634342-0-9

Printing by Cascade Printing Co., Corvallis, Or.
Cover design by Steven Burkey

 recycled paper

Contents

Dedications • 7

A "Herstory" • 9

Kitchen Creativity • 13

♥ Recipes ♥

Dressings and Marinades • 15

Soups • 35

Salads • 63

Quiches • 107

Breads and Muffins • 133

A Couple of Entrées • 163

～ || ～

Epilogue • 175

Index • 177

> "gourmet: Any food that is cooked conscientiously with intelligence, with great care, with enthusiasm. If it's done with your heart and soul, it's bound to be gourmet."
>
> Craig Claiborne

Dedications

In memory of
Leslie Fieber,
who had a way with
simple soup and corn muffins
that cannot be matched.
I see
you smiling.

My profound gratitude and appreciation to all who helped make this book a reality:

Robert, whose unfailing support and encouragement kept me going - along with the late-night back rubs.

Sally Daly, Barbara Ginsburg, Judi Kloper, Chris Peterson, Jo Roach, Michael Sherwin, and Jan Weir for editing, advice, creative input, encouragement & friendship.

Dawn, Leslie, Vibeke, Lynn, Terry, Judy, Chris, Jennifer, Sarah, Dave, Oceana, Kathy & Mico - the Café crew. Thanks for taking care of business so I could write this book!

A dedication to you — The Cook

A certain peace and an encouraging order can be attained in preparing and enjoying a delicious meal. Do it for yourself as often as you can — you deserve it! Do it for your friends and you'll always have some. Do it for your family and they'll know you care in a way that words cannot describe.

Nothing is better than a steaming pot of homemade soup, warm bread fresh from the oven, and a crisp salad full of fresh, colorful vegetables. It can convince even the most ultra-ambitious to take a nourishing — necessary — pause from a hectic day. Everyone needs to sit back, relax, and savor both food and the time to enjoy it.

The recipes that follow are composed of simple ingredients: grains, vegetables, pasta, and herbs. They are close to the earth and brimming with the beauty of nature. May you enjoy using them as much as I've enjoyed writing them down for you.

Francie O'Shea
October 1992

A "Herstory"

Café Croissant was a seedling of a dream in a cozy corner of my mind when I started my home business, Dial-A-Croissant, in the autumn of 1983. Dial-A-Croissant boasted "freshly-baked croissants delivered to your doorstep for Sunday morning breakfast and brunch."

It didn't take long to build up a comfortable customer base and, in no time at all, the hours increased with the clientele. I was still working virtually alone when our local newspaper, the Gazette-Times, decided to find out which local bakery offered the best croissants in town. Dial-A-Croissant won! The ensuing feature article on the front page of the GT food section set Dial-A-Croissant's phone in perpetual motion. Orders poured in; local restaurants and coffee shops wanted wholesale accounts. I hired my first employees and onward we flew, making, baking and delivering croissants. It was an exciting yet somewhat terrifying time, but I wouldn't trade it for the world!

I wasn't suprised that Dial-A-Croissant was voted the best. I've always approached baking as an art form, and croissants really lend themselves to art since they're a soft, lovely creation shaped with your hands. They're food for the eyes and soul, as well as for the body. Only the finest ingredients go into my croissants. It's really quite a short list: fresh, unsalted butter, unbleached flour, milk, yeast, and a little sugar and salt. That's it. After just the right amount of tender mixing, buttering, folding and rolling, each croissant is formed (some are filled with fresh fruit, nuts, cheese or chocolate) and then left to rise. When ready, they are gently brushed with a whole egg/milk "wash" and baked to a lovely golden brown. Their layered edges puff up and separate in the authentic puff-pastry fashion. A true work of art!

Within a few months, I had a staff of four helping with the various stages of croissant production. Our home kitchen became a full-time bakery but my husband, Robert, an easy-going soul, never complained. (He was as thrilled as I was with the success of my new business... not to mention having fresh croissants for breakfast every morning!)

Besides tending to our ever-expanding wholesale accounts, we advertized our way into people's minds. When a special occasion arose or a friend needed cheering up - or just a special treat — people would think of Dial-A-Croissant's unique service. Our fragrant boxes of warm croissants have cheered, surprised, and made countless special occasions all the more special. (They still do!)

In the summer of 1984, we started selling our croissants at the Farmers' Markets in Albany and Corvallis. I've always loved farmers' markets. In fact, before starting my business, I would take the excess fresh vegetables, flowers, and herbs from our large, organic home garden to sell there. When I approached the organizers of the Markets about selling food (which was not done at that time, although it's quite common now) they were willing and encouraging, so we gave it a try. What a fun, fantastic, and lucrative experience it turned out to be! Our bright rainbow-colored umbrella became a beacon, leading customers back each week. Soon we were selling everything we could bring. (You should have seen our station wagon, stuffed to the brim with bulging pink bakery boxes!)

It was during the Farmers' Markets of '84 and '85 that the dream of Café Croissant began to evolve beyond the embryonic stage. During this time we expanded our line of baked goods to include cinnamon and pecan rolls, little orange poppyseed cakes, muffins, brownies, and small breads. We also started serving coffee. We developed a customer base of "regulars" who stopped by to see us every week at our stand to enjoy a fresh pastry and a cup of coffee for breakfast while they shopped for fresh produce.

Meanwhile, back at home, Robert and I were beginning to feel like campers in a bakery. Our house was filled with baking trays and stacks of bakery boxes. Our kitchen was coated with a fine dusting of flour, and a 20-quart mixer took up an entire counter. Ovens had taken over the kitchen, laundry room, and garage. When we opened our refrigerator, all we saw were baking ingredients. Also, we were beginning to tire of having workers in our kitchen day and night. The time had come to find Dial-A-Croissant a home of its own.

I'd been eyeing an empty storefront on 5th. street for months. It was downtown, on the university side, near the City and County offices and courthouse, and right next to the main city bus stop. The location was right, the size was right, the price was right. Dial-A-Croissant moved in in October of 1985 and I immediately started serious plans for turning my dream of a café into reality.

All through that winter and the following spring

we searched for restaurant equipment. Most of it we bought locally, including my favorites. First was the 8'x4' solid cherry baker's table, which we found in Philomath. It's still the centerpiece of our kitchen. Our "designer pink" gas stove, on which we cook all our soups and pastas, was "bought" from a person in Lewisburg. The price: 1½ dozen filled croissants - delivered. Finally, our Montague gas convection oven - the heart of our kitchen - was purchased from a foreign man who refused to talk business with me because I was a woman. Since I really wanted the oven, we played his game. Robert did the talking and I got an incredible deal!

In February, 1986, we started remodeling. Local craftspeople turned a bakery into the café of my dreams - where customers would feel comfortable about lingering over their breakfasts and papers before delving into a busy day or sliding into a lazy weekend. I think we achieved our goal through the rich handcrafted wood, cream-colored walls, sparkling brass and glass, and black and white floors.

Meanwhile, I was in the kitchen testing recipes, developing a menu, organizing the staff and dealing with countless details. A new crew of counter people joined the kitchen staff, and we opened for business on May 10, 1986.

Since then we've continued to nourish the bodies and moods of our customers through our commitment to serve the finest foods we are capable of preparing, and maintaining a comfortable inviting ambiance. Many have been coming in since, literally, the first day we opened. They are just as responsible as our food, space, and staff for making the Café what it is today. Thanks to every one of you!

Kitchen Creativity

Every recipe is a marvelous little nugget of information. It tells you what ingredients you will need, guides you through the process and acquaints you with some tried and true food combinations. Don't burden your already overtaxed mind when you stagger home after a long day and hear, once again, "What are we having for dinner?" Pick up this cookbook and whip up a quick, simple and nutritious meal. Better yet, have a delicious leftover squirreled away for just such a day. (All these recipes make fabulous serve-again meals.)

On the less-stressful days the fun can begin. Pull out your favorite cookbook (this one, I hope) and go for it! No one knows what really turns you on - foodwise - better than you do. Family and friends will look forward to seeing what you create next. They'll congratulate a success and forgive a mistake, and they'll no doubt enjoy eating both! Plus, you can count on them for plenty of valuable "feed-back." (No pun intended!)

Creative cooking is intriguing and effortless when you get into the right frame of mind. It's an ongoing process. Every time you cook, think about what you could do to the recipe to improve it, to make it more interesting for you and your family. Take notes, it's ok to write in the spaces I left for notes, or even in the margins. Pretty soon you will naturally be cooking more intuitively, creating new and distinctive dishes. Good luck!

"Dining is
and always was
a great
artistic
opportunity."

Frank Lloyd Wright

Dressings and Marinades

- An Introduction 17
- Vinaigrette Dressing 25
- Parmesan Vinaigrette Dressing 26
- Creamy Italian Dressing 27
- Oriental Dressing 28
- Honey Mustard Dressing 29
- Blue Cheese Dressing 30
- Sweet Hot Mustard 31
- Pesto 32
- Teriyaki Sauce 33

> "'Tis an ill cook
> that cannot lick
> his own fingers."
>
> — William Shakespeare

Dressings and Marinades

Next time you are in the grocery store, notice the assortment of bottled salad dressings, sauces, mustards and marinades waiting to be purchased. The choice is enormous! You could spend years and a lot of money trying them all. But why bother? For a little time and a lot less money you can have a lovely bottle of dressing on your kitchen table that will taste better, be exactly what you want, and be made by your own hands. Not only is it something to be proud of, it's guaranteed to delight your family and friends.

A sharp knife, wire whisk and bowl are the only tools you really need, but a blender and food processor will make the job easier still. To make Sweet-Hot Mustard you'll need a double boiler, easily improvised with a small pot inside a larger one. Most of these tools are available in any kitchen, even a minimally-equipped one.

The most important factor is the quality, freshness and flavor of your ingredients. Use only the best! This does not necessarily mean the most expensive, although there is truth in the adage "you get what you pay for." Read labels, taste-test and observe. Over time you will develop an eye for fresh ingredients and top quality.

Vinegars

There are many delicious vinegars to choose from to make your dressings.

Red and White Wine Vinegar: Pungent and aromatic, these all-purpose vinegars are great in vinaigrette and other dressings.

continued →

Basalmic Vinegar: This pungent, slightly sweet and rich wine vinegar comes from Italy. It's aged in wooden barrels a few to a dozen years, becoming sweeter the longer it is aged. Adds a distinctive flavor to your dressings. Experiment with this one!

Apple Cider Vinegar: A tangy vinegar made from apples (of course!) and great in dressings for fruit salads.

Malt Vinegar: This mild vinegar is made from malted barley and is used mainly by the British as a topping for fish and chips.

Rice Vinegar: The many varieties of Japanese rice vinegar range in color from the mildest white to a very sweet purple-black vinegar. The clear white to light amber rice vinegar, readily available in our country, is pleasantly mild in flavor. Great in dressings and marinades and wonderful on rice salads and vegetables.

Distilled White Vinegar: Made from a grain-alcohol mixture, this is too harsh for dressings. Can be used in canning and preserving.

Your choice in vinegars is endless when you consider flavored vinegars for dressings and marinades. Two popular varieties are herb vinegars and fruit vinegars.

Herb Vinegar

1. Lightly bruise 1 cup of leaves from whatever fresh herb you choose. Tarragon is the most popular, but basil, thyme, and rosemary are delicious, too.
2. Place in a heat-proof jar and pour 2 cups of your favorite vinegar, heated to just below the boiling point, over the herbs.

continued →

3. Seal the bottle and let the herbs steep for about 2 weeks, shaking the bottle occasionally.
4. Pour the vinegar through a cheesecloth or coffee filter into a pretty jar with a fresh sprig of the herb in it. Cork the bottle and decorate with an attractive label. A perfect gift! Store in a cool, dark place.

Fruit Vinegar

1. In a sterilized jar soak 1 lb. ripe berries or soft fruit in 3 cups mild, light vinegar. Use any soft fruit or berry. Raspberry is a favorite, but peach, blueberry, and apricot are excellent, too. Good vinegars to use are rice or white wine.
2. Seal the jar and leave in a cool place for 2 weeks shaking daily.
3. Pour the fruit and vinegar through a cheesecloth or coffee filter, pressing the fruit to extract as much juice as possible.
4. Add 3-4 Tbs. of sugar, and simmer the vinegar for 5-10 minutes. Strain into sterilized jars and cork. Stamp with a pretty label stating the type of fruit and vinegar used, your name, and the date. Makes a lovely gift! Store in a cool place.

Oils

Here are just a few of the many oils available. To decide which to use, simply go with what tastes best to you. Simple? Yes and no. Make a point to buy small bottles of different oils to experiment with

continued →

in your dressings. When eating out, sample different dressings and ask about the ingredients. Soon you will have developed a basis for choosing and an assortment of bright, flavorful oils to use in your dressings and marinades.

- Canola Oil: This good, all-purpose oil is the lowest in saturated fats and mild in taste. Used in all realms of cooking, it's fine for dressings.
- Sesame Oil: We use this oil in many of our dressings. It's light yellow in color and has a mild, nutty flavor. Especially good for high-temperature cooking.
- Oriental Sesame Oil: Pale to dark amber in color, rich and pungent in flavor. Always use in small amounts so it will complement- not overpower- the other flavors in the dish.
- Corn Oil: A good, all-purpose oil. However, it's slightly harsh in flavor so is not recommended for salads.
- Sunflower Oil: Another light all-purpose oil, fine for dressings and marinades.
- Soy Oil: This oil is almost flavorless, fine for dressings.
- Peanut Oil: A good salad oil, light and nutty in flavor.
- Walnut Oil: This oil has a wonderful flavor and aroma and is more distinctive in your salads. Somewhat more expensive than the other oils, it's worth the price and can be used sparingly with good results.
- Hot Oil: Made from sesame oil heated with crushed, dried hot chili peppers. Spicy hot with an orange-red hue. Adds personality (and "heat") to salads. Use sparingly.

continued →

Olive Oil: It's interesting (and confusing) just how many different kinds of olive oil are available today. Should you buy virgin, extra virgin or extra extra virgin, cold-drawn or cold-pressed, filtered or unfiltered, refined or unrefined? Or how about extra fine, superfine, semi-fine, regular, pure or sansa (from the second pressing)? To make things even more confusing, different countries use different terms to describe their own varieties of olive oil.

The best oil to use for cooking is unrefined oil that comes from the first pressing, which has been conducted at a low temperature using high-grade olives. This can be hard to discern from the label but the terms "cold-pressed" or "cold-drawn" and "extra virgin" are good clues.

I choose my olive oil by color and taste. I prefer oil made from fully ripe olives which is golden in color and has a full, rich flavor. Green olive oils are made from partially-ripe olives and tend to have a sharper taste, which many prefer. A pungent, dark, unrefined oil is delicious in pesto. Use a lighter oil in dressings for delicate vegetable salads. Pasta dishes can handle a full-flavored olive oil.

I suggest you buy several olive oils, try them in different dishes, and decide which brands and types you like best. Always have some on hand as it's an essential part of a well-equipped kitchen.

Keep all your oils refrigerated after they are open.

continued →

Some, like olive, stay fresh longer and can be stored in a cool, dark place. However, refrigerating is more dependable and guarantees a fresh, non-rancid oil when you need it. Olive oil will partially solidify when refrigerated but will become liquid again at room temperature. Run hot water over the bottle or stand it in a pan of hot water to hasten the process.

Other Ingredients

Lemon juice: Lemon juice can replace vinegar in dressings but be sure to use less. Because lemon juice is stronger and more acidic, it can be overbearing in amounts equal to vinegar. I include a little fresh lemon juice in my dressings and marinades to add the "bite" and freshness it so beautifully gives to food. Always use fresh lemon juice; the processed version is unsatisfactory in flavor. Lemons keep very well (a month or more) in the refrigerator. Keep a couple in your kitchen at all times. One medium-large lemon yields about 4 Tbs. of juice.

Garlic: Fresh is always best, but it's a must when making dressings and marinades. The difference in taste is quite obvious between fresh and dried garlic. Invest in a good garlic press to make using it easier. Fresh garlic is less expensive and widely available. Pick firm plump heads with dry skin.

continued →

Avoid garlic with shriveled cloves or any damage. Store in an open container in a cool, dark place. Garlic will keep for 6 weeks or more.

Herbs: Fresh herbs, in comparison to dried, are more delicate and immediate in flavor so they taste better. Dried herbs work well in dressings if the flavors have had time to blend and heighten. I've used the figures for dried herbs in the recipes since they are more readily available, but if you grow or have a source for fresh herbs, by all means use them. They are interchangeable but the amount must be converted. When using fresh, use 3 times the amount of dried herb called for in the recipe.
    ♥ Example: ½ tsp. basil = 1½ tsp. <u>fresh</u> basil

Mustard: Dijon mustard is the most famous prepared mustard, originating in Dijon, France. It is made with ground black mustard seed, salt, spices, vinegar, and wine. Nothing more, nothing less. There are many variations on the theme and they are distinguished by the label: Dijon <u>style</u>. Characteristic is the pungent, tangy, almost hot mustard flavor. Delicious with meats and poultry and in sauces and dressings. The mustard we use at the Café is imported from France. Our favorite (famous!) mustard is the Café's own Sweet Hot Mustard (p. 31). Different from Dijon, it's mild, slightly sweet, and rich. Very versatile, it's used in much of our cooking, and it's fabulous on sandwiches.

continued ⟶

Soy Sauce: Also known as tamari or shoyu, it's made by adding salt to cooked soybeans (and sometimes roasted wheat) and letting it ferment. The longer the fermentation, the smoother the soy sauce. The more expensive Oriental brands may be much tastier, especially if they are aged, with the richness in flavor far outweighing the extra expense. These brands are generally less salty, too. You can also purchase a low-sodium "lite" soy sauce, which has had up to half the salt removed. Just don't get this mixed up with "light" soy sauce that is paler in color, less intensely flavored, but is actually saltier! Read labels and compare brands to make a savvy choice.

Ginger Root: A spicy, very pleasant flavor and aroma that goes well with sweet and/or savory foods. It is now widely available, so use fresh whenever possible. Whole pieces of ginger root are called hands. Choose hands that have smooth skin and a fresh, spicy fragrance. Fresh, unpeeled ginger root will keep for a week in the refrigerator or 1-2 months in the freezer. Dried ground ginger is better for baking and also can be substituted for fresh in dressings. Buy the most aromatic in small amounts and store in a tightly-sealed jar in a cool, dark cupboard.

★ note: 1/2 tsp. ground ginger = 1 1/2 tsp. minced fresh ginger

Vinaigrette Dressing
Makes 2½ cups

A "must have" for your salad making. You can use store-bought in a pinch but this is so much better and really quite easy to make. This is my favorite recipe. Feel free to make it yours by adding different herbs, more or less garlic, omitting the salt, etc. Just be sure to keep the oil-to-vinegar ratio the same. Make a double (or even triple!) batch. It will keep a few weeks in the refrigerator in a covered glass jar.

½ cup red wine vinegar
¼ cup chopped onion
2 cloves garlic, minced
2 Tbs. Dijon mustard
1 Tbs. honey
4 Tbs. fresh lemon juice

1 tsp. salt
1 tsp. white pepper
⅛ tsp. each: basil, dill, tarragon, marjoram, thyme
1 cup vegetable oil
½ cup olive oil

1. Put everything but oils in your blender or food processor. Mix until smooth.
2. Combine oils, and, while machine is running, pour in slowly through the open top or feed tube. Mix until dressing is smooth and thick.

♥ note: This can be made in a bowl using a wire whisk to stir. Finely mince both the onions and garlic. Whisk in oil slowly, until thick.

Parmesan Vinaigrette
makes 1¾ cups

Our most popular salad dressing! It's a cinch to make once you've got a supply of Vinaigrette waiting faithfully in the refrigerator. Store in a tightly covered glass jar in the refrigerator. It will keep a few weeks.

    1½ cups Vinaigrette dressing (p. 25)
    ¼ cup grated Parmesan cheese

Just stir it all together. <u>That's</u> it!

. . . .

notes ♥

Creamy Italian Dressing
makes 3 cups

A creamy version of our Vinaigrette dressing. It's easy to whip up for those occasions when a creamy dressing will complement your meal: poached fish, baked chicken or even a barbecue. A delicious dressing on fresh greens (of course!), it's also delightful as a dressing on potato salad or fresh shrimp salad. During the summer we pour it over fresh-from-the-garden ripe red tomatoes or steamed green beans. Sigh... Keeps a week or so refrigerated in a tightly covered glass jar.

1 (8-oz.) package cream cheese, at room temperature
1 cup Vinaigrette dressing (p.25)
1 cup Half & Half or milk
1 tsp. honey
1 tsp. Dijon mustard
2 Tbs. red wine vinegar
1 clove garlic, minced
1/8 tsp. paprika
2 Tbs. chopped fresh chives or 1 Tbs. dried chopped chives
- ♥ note: If chives are not available substitute minced green onion greens or fresh parsley.

Put everything but chives in your blender or food processor. Mix until smooth. Stir in chives.

- ★ note: This can be made by hand. In a large bowl stir softened cream cheese until smooth. Add remaining ingredients. Blend well.

Oriental Dressing
Makes 2 cups

This is the dressing we use on our Far East — influenced salads: Oriental Sesame Pasta, Chicken Szechuan, and Chicken Sesame Rice. But there is no need to stop there! Try it on your favorite stir-fry, as a topping over hot brown rice, a dip for tempura, a marinade for seafood or chicken, or even a salad dressing on fresh greens. Very versatile (whew... an understatement!) and delicious. It will keep a few weeks, refrigerated in a covered glass jar.

¼ cup rice vinegar
¼ cup Teriyaki sauce (p.33)
3 Tbs. soy sauce
1 Tbs. Dijon mustard
2 tsp. fresh lemon juice

1 large clove garlic, minced
2 Tbs. minced parsley
¼ tsp. cayenne pepper
¼ cup Oriental sesame oil 🍓
¾ cup vegetable oil

1. Put everything but oils in your blender or food processor. Mix until smooth.
2. Combine oils, and, while machine is running, pour in slowly through the open top or feed tube. Mix until dressing is smooth and thick.

♥ note: this can be made in a bowl with a whisk. <u>Finely</u> mince (or press) garlic. Whisk in oil slowly.

🍓 Oriental sesame oil is made from roasted sesame seeds. It is pale to dark amber in color and the flavor is rich and pungent.

Honey Mustard Dressing
Makes 3½ cups

This dressing is in its heyday right now. It's difficult to keep it in stock at the Café! Use as a dressing on fresh greens and also as a dip for fresh veggies or as a sauce for fried fish and chicken. It will keep for a week or two in a covered jar in the refrigerator.

1 cup Sweet Hot Mustard (p. 31)
1 cup mayonnaise
1 Tbs. honey
1 tsp. Dijon mustard
3 Tbs. minced green onions
3 Tbs. minced fresh parsley
¼ - ½ tsp. salt (to taste)
¼ tsp. white or black pepper
¾ cup Half & Half or milk

In a large bowl mix together all ingredients until thoroughly combined.

Black pepper is ground from peppercorns that are picked unripe and dried in the sun to develop color and flavor. White pepper is ground from mature peppercorns, soaked in water to remove the outer coating and dried. Both are similar in flavor. Use white pepper in custards, cream soups, or any light dishes that black pepper would discolor. Buy whole berries and store in the freezer. Grind as you need for the best flavor.

Blue Cheese Dressing
Makes 3½ cups

A delicious, easy to make Blue cheese dressing. Blue cheese lovers - this one's for you! Use on fresh greens, as a dip for fresh veggies or as a sauce over steamed veggies. My husband Robert spoons it on his baked potato - to each his own! Refrigerate in a covered glass jar for a week or so.

½ lb. blue cheese, crumbled
2 cups mayonnaise
1 tsp. Dijon mustard
1½ tsp. Worcestershire sauce
½ tsp. Tabasco sauce
1 small clove garlic, minced
¼ tsp. salt
¼ tsp. black pepper
½ cup buttermilk
½ cup Half & Half or milk
2 tsp. poppy seeds

In a large bowl, mix together all ingredients (except buttermilk, Half & Half and poppyseeds) until well blended. (It will still be a little chunky because of the crumbled blue cheese.) Stir in buttermilk and Half & Half. Mix well. Add poppyseeds for color and contrast if desired.

Worcestershire sauce was developed in India by the English. It contains vinegar, molasses, anchovies, salt, onions, garlic, chili peppers, soy sauce, tamarind, lime, etc.

Sweet Hot Mustard
Makes 4 cups

This is the mustard that Café Croissant is famous for. It's a slightly sweet, mild mustard that has a nice "bite" to it. Delicious with anything that you'd put mustard on, it's absolutely out of this world on a Turkey Croissant sandwich! Sweet hot mustard will keep for several weeks refrigerated in a covered glass jar, so go ahead and make a large batch. It makes a wonderful gift, dressed up in a classy jar with your own label or tucked into a basket with some cheese, bread, fruit, and wine.

6 eggs
1 cup white wine vinegar
1 cup dry mustard
½ cup granulated sugar
⅓ cup honey

1. In a large bowl, using a wire whisk, beat all ingredients together until thoroughly mixed.
2. Transfer to the top of a glass or stainless steel double boiler. Cook over, not in, boiling water whisking every few minutes until thick, 10-15 min.
   ♥ note: do not let mustard boil - it will become bitter. Reduce heat, if necessary.
3. When thick, whisk energetically to fluff it up. Cool and refrigerate.

Pesto
makes 2 cups

The secret to having fresh Pesto throughout the year without paying the exorbitant prices at the gourmet counter is (of course!) to make your own. Make it in the summer when basil is fresh and in abundance in your garden or at the Farmers' Market. Make some to enjoy immediately but also put some away for later - Pesto freezes beautifully! Prepare and freeze without the nuts and cheese; add them after thawing. Or freeze it ready-to-use, in small amounts, according to how much you use at a time. Pesto will keep for several weeks refrigerated in a tightly covered glass jar with a thin layer of vegetable oil on the surface. We use Pesto in our Pesto Pasta and Café Pizza. It's also delicious as a sauce for hot pasta (just toss together) or as a spread on sandwiches and crusty french bread!

3 cups fresh basil leaves, packed
1 cup fresh parsley packed
1/2 cup pine nuts or walnuts
3/4 cup grated Parmesan cheese
3 large cloves garlic
1/4 - 1/2 tsp. salt
3/4 cup olive oil

Menu Suggestion: core and hollow ripe cherry tomatoes. Fill each with Pesto and top with a toasted pine nut!

Combine everything in your blender or food processor. Mix until smooth. Scrape sides with a spatula to help combine.

Teriyaki Sauce
makes 2 cups

It's incredibly easy to make your own delicious, gourmet teriyaki sauce - at a fraction of what you'd pay for the "good stuff" at the grocery store. This is the sauce we use to marinate the chicken for our salads and as an ingredient in our Oriental dressing. It can also be used as a dip for tempura or fresh veggies. At home, a personal favorite is sliced tofu marinated in teriyaki sauce and barbecued on the grill. Fantastic! Teriyaki sauce, refrigerated in a covered glass jar, will keep several weeks.

1 cup soy sauce
½ cup brown sugar
¼ cup minced onion
¼ cup minced fresh parsley
1-2 cloves garlic, minced
1 tsp. Dijon mustard
1 Tbs. rice vinegar
1 Tbs. minced fresh ginger
   or 1 tsp. ground ginger
2 Tbs. Oriental sesame oil
2 Tbs. vegetable oil

★ note: For a less salty teriyaki sauce use an aged Oriental soy sauce called shoyu or tamari. It has a much richer flavor and is not nearly as salty.

Put everything (including oils) in your blender or food processor. Mix until smooth.
   ♥ note: If making by hand, allow to sit for about 4 hours so the flavors have a chance to combine. Then strain the sauce, removing the larger pieces.

> "Give me neither poverty nor riches; feed me with foods convenient for me."
>
> Proverbs 30:8

Soups

- ★ An Introduction 36
- ★ Robert's Chili 39
- ★ Country Vegetable Barley 42
- ★ Broccoli Cheddar 44
- ★ Minestrone 46
- ★ Lentil 48
- ★ U.S. Senate Bean 50
- ★ Tomato Tortellini 52
- ★ Old Fashioned Turkey Barley 54
- ★ Mexi-Corn Chowder 56
- ★ Potato Cheddar 58
- ★ Santa Fe Cheddar 60

"Soup is comfort food. It makes you feel as good as it tastes."

Soups

Making soup is simple. Mainly one pot productions, these soups take less than half an hour to prepare, not including simmering time. Soup making can be a relaxing endeavor. Spend time leaning over the pot, looking, stirring, thinking, and tasting. Make it thicker and heartier by pureeing a portion or adding mashed potatoes. Thin by adding more broth, water, or milk. Adjust the seasonings, adding a little more of the herbs, salt, pepper, or another clove of garlic. If you make soup often enough, you will become quite adept at the process and soup making will become instinctive.

Two terms that are often misunderstood are simmer and sauté.

Simmer: To gently cook food in liquid at a temperature low enough that tiny bubbles just begin to break the surface. This happens at around 185°F. Simmered food will cook more slowly, preventing the ingredients from overcooking and breaking up.

Sauté: To rapidly cook food in a small amount of oil or butter over direct heat. This is the first step in most soup making, bringing out the flavor of the ingredients.

If you are on a salt-restricted diet or just prefer to eat less salt, these recipes can be easily adapted. Use less salt (or none) during the sauté phase. After you have completed the soup, taste it. Does the flavor need to be enhanced? Lemon juice can be used in place of salt. Add a little and taste again. (In a cream

continued →

or milk-based soup, lemon juice could make the milk separate and look curdled.) You can also add more of the herbs and some freshly ground pepper to spice it up. Feel free to substitute your favorite vegetable oil for the butter (which contains salt unless you use "unsalted") in any of these recipes as they are interchangeable.

Since these soups aren't made with fatty meat or fatty stock, it's possible to lower, or even eliminate, the fat in many of them. There are several ways to accomplish this. The simplest is to spoon off the fat, then blot up the remaining shiny fat layer on the surface of the soup with a paper towel. Another method is a special pitcher that pours the soup out through a spout in the bottom, below the fat layer. Or refrigerate the completed soup and, when it becomes cold, remove the solidified fat on the surface. My favorite method is to adapt the recipe. This will give you a virtually fat-free soup, provided you add no fatty ingredients like meat or cheese. Instead of using the butter or oil called for, use a vegetable oil spray to coat your pan. Cook your vegetables, covered, until tender. Keep the heat slightly lower and stir often. If it sticks, add a little water. Any potatoes or barley that are usually sautéed with the veggies would tend to stick and burn using this method, so they should be boiled until tender and added later. Proceed normally with the rest of the recipe.

You can make delicious hearty soup for pennies a serving. Try the Mexi-Corn Chowder, Lentil, Country Vegetable Barley, Robert's Chili, and Minestrone during cost-cutting times. You will still feel well-

continued ⟶

fed and content.

Most of the soups included here are very hearty and stand alone as the main course. A fresh salad (pgs. 64 - 105) and some warm bread (pgs. 133 - 161) complete a meal that is as nourishing as it is delicious.

Most soups freeze well. Make extra and freeze for a quick meal to serve on one those exceptionally hectic days we all experience from time to time. Freeze in a plastic container with a close-fitting lid. Fill only 3/4 full to give room for expansion as the soup freezes. Soup will keep in the freezer for several months. Defrost in the microwave or overnight in the refrigerator.

Note ♥ A Hint About Milk-Based Soups

After adding milk, light-cream (Half & Half), or cream to a soup, never allow it to boil. This will cause a milk-based soup to separate. After adding the milk towards the end of the recipe, bring the soup up to serving temperature over medium heat. (The soup will be hot and steam slightly but no bubbles will break the surface.) Watch closely and stir often. When hot, reduce heat to very low and serve at once. The soup can be transferred to a double-boiler to keep it hot for an extended time.

Cream or milk-based soups tend to separate and appear curdled after freezing and reheating, so I don't recommend freezing them.

Robert's Chili
6 generous servings

Simply called Chili when we serve it at the Café, I'd like to dedicate it here to my husband, Robert, who showed me great chili can be made without meat. When Robert and I met during the '70's, he had quite a repertoire of signature dishes — most of them revolving around beans! We lived simply in those days and learned to do exciting things with simple foods. This recipe was born of those times and, although it's been enhanced a little through the years, it's virtually the same lovely recipe that Robert created.

It's a rich veggie-laden chili. An important difference between our chili and most others is the beans. We use only pinto beans - never thick-skinned kidney beans. Pinto beans are richer, softer, and tastier — truly an all-around better bean.

1¼ c. dry pinto beans
½ tsp. salt   OR 2 (15 oz) cans pinto beans
2 bay leaves
6 cups water

4 Tbs. vegetable oil
3-4 cloves garlic, minced
1 large onion, chopped
2 stalks celery, sliced
1 green bell pepper, seeded and sliced
1 red bell pepper, seeded and sliced
1 jalapeño pepper, seeded and sliced
½ tsp. salt

continued →

(Robert's Chili, continued)

1 large tomato, seeded and chopped
½ cup thinly-sliced green onion
½ cup chopped fresh parsley
¼ cup chopped fresh cilantro, optional
1 cup fresh or frozen corn, optional
1-2 Tbs. chili powder
2 tsp. cumin
1 tsp. oregano
¼ tsp. black pepper
⅛ tsp. cayenne

2-4 Tbs. tomato paste
1 (15-oz.) can tomato sauce
4 cups water (if using canned beans)

♥note: Skip step 1 if using canned beans.

1. Soak beans in 4 cups water at least 4 hours (or overnight). Drain. In a saucepan (3qt.) combine soaked beans, salt, bay leaves, and 6 cups water. Bring to a boil, reduce heat to medium, and cook, covered, until beans are soft and tender, about 1 hour. (Add more water as the beans cook. You'll want about 4 cups of liquid in the pot when beans are done.)
2. In a large, wide pot (6qt.) cook garlic in oil until lightly browned. Add onions, celery, peppers, and salt (and bay leaves if using canned beans). Sauté 12 minutes over medium heat, stirring often. Add remaining veggies and spices and cook until onions and celery are tender, 8-10 minutes. (Stir often as the spices have a tendency to stick and burn. Reduce heat to medium-low and/or

continued →

(Robert's Chili, continued)

add a little more vegetable oil if necessary. Sautéing the spices helps develop their flavor.)

3. Stir tomato sauce and 2 Tbs. tomato paste into the veggies. Cook a few minutes until saucey and hot.
4. Add cooked beans and water (or canned beans and 4 cups fresh water) to veggies in pot. Bring to a healthy boil over high heat, stirring often. Reduce heat to low and simmer, covered, for 30 minutes, stirring occasionally.
5. Time to lean over the pot, taste and think. Does it need more chili powder? Cumin? Garlic? Salt? Is it hot enough? Cayenne will "heat" it up - add a _little_ at a time. Too thin? Puree some of the soup and stir back in or just simmer, uncovered, a while longer. Too thick? Easy - add water. Add the remaining 2 Tbs. tomato paste for a richer, more "tomatoey" chili. When you have it just right (wait - don't eat it yet, relax for a few minutes), simmer, covered, over very low heat until ready to serve. Remove bay leaves.

> Serving Suggestion: Garnish with shredded Cheddar and a pinch of sliced green onion. Serve with Garden Veggie Pasta and warm Cornbread.

Chili powder is a blend of spices created in the American Southwest during this century. It contains dried, ground sweet (paprika) and hot (cayenne) red peppers, oregano, cumin, garlic, coriander, cloves, and salt. You can buy chili powder in varying degrees of "hotness" from blistering to bland. If you do burn your mouth, drink beer or milk to relieve the stinging. Store chili powder in a sealed glass jar in a cool dark cupboard.

Country Vegetable Barley
6 generous servings

This is a hearty vegetable soup. All the veggies should be chopped into large bite-sized pieces to give it a chunky texture and appearance.

- 3 Tbs. butter or vegetable oil
- 1-2 cloves garlic
- 3 Tbs. raw barley
- 1 large onion, chopped
- 1 cup chopped broccoli
- 3 stalks celery, sliced
- 3 carrots, halved lengthwise and sliced
- 1 potato, chopped (peeled or not - your choice)
- 2 bay leaves
- ½ tsp. salt

- 1 green bell pepper, seeded and chopped
- 1 small zucchini, halved lengthwise and sliced

- ¼ cup fresh or frozen corn
- ¼ cup fresh or frozen peas
- ¼ cup chopped fresh parsley
- ¼ cup thinly-sliced green onions
- ½ tsp. *each* basil and marjoram
- ¼ tsp. *each* rosemary and oregano
- ¼ tsp. black pepper

- 1 (29-oz) can tomato sauce
- 2-3 cups water
- 2-4 Tbs. tomato paste

continued ⟶

(Country Vegetable Barley, continued)

1. In a large wide pot (6 qt.) cook garlic in melted butter or oil until lightly browned. Add barley, onions, broccoli, celery, carrots, potato, bay leaves, and salt and cook, covered, over medium heat for 10 minutes, stirring often. Add green pepper and zucchini and sauté, uncovered, for 7 minutes more. Add remaining veggies, herbs, and black pepper and sauté 4-5 minutes more. (Veggies will be tender and barley still a little chewy when done.)
2. Stir in tomato sauce, 2 cups water, and tomato paste. Bring to a boil over high heat, reduce heat to low and simmer, covered, for 30 minutes, stirring occasionally.
3. Add the remaining cup of water to thin the soup if necessary. Taste and adjust seasonings. Reduce heat to very low and gently simmer until ready to serve. Remove bay leaves before serving.

> **Serving Suggestion:** Scrumptious served with any freshly-baked bread but do try the Irish Soda Bread. Slice it thinly, toast and spread with Garlic-Parmesan Butter (recipe below). Add a salad of fresh greens... Enjoy!

Garlic-Parmesan Butter
- ½ cup (1 stick) softened butter
- 1 clove garlic, finely-minced or pressed
- 1 Tbs. grated Parmesan cheese
- ♥ mix together well

Broccoli Cheddar
4-6 servings

Everyone's favorite!

3 Tbs. butter or vegetable oil
1-2 cloves garlic, minced
2 cups separated broccoli florets
remaining broccoli stalk, finely-chopped
1 small onion, finely-chopped
1 stalk celery, finely-chopped
1 small carrot, finely-chopped
1 small green bell pepper, finely-chopped
1/4 tsp. salt
1 bay leaf
1/4 tsp. each paprika and white pepper
1/16 tsp. each cayenne and nutmeg

> **Variation**
> Use cauliflower instead of broccoli and call it: Cheesy Cauliflower Soup! ♥ Nice ♥

2/3 cup flour
1 Tbs. cornstarch
3 1/2 cups homemade chicken broth
    or 2 (14-oz.) cans chicken broth
    or 3 1/2 cups water (see note)
4 cups (1 lb.) shredded Cheddar cheese
2 cups Half & Half or milk

♥ note: When using water instead of chicken broth it's a good idea to increase the seasonings. Use a rounded 1/4 tsp. of paprika & white pepper, 1/8 tsp. cayenne & nutmeg, and an extra bay leaf. Add more salt, if desired, at the end when you taste to adjust seasonings.

continued →

(Broccoli Cheddar, continued)

1. In a large, wide pot cook garlic in oil until lightly browned. Add remaining veggies, bay leaf, and salt; sauté 10-12 minutes over medium heat. Stir in spices and seasonings; cook 1-2 minutes. (Veggies will be tender when done.)
2. In a small bowl stir together flour and cornstarch. Add half of the chicken broth or water to the veggies. Cook over medium heat until hot but not boiling and stir in the flour/cornstarch mixture, a little at a time, until all has been added and the veggie mixture is bubbly and thick.
3. Add the remaining chicken broth or water, a little at a time, stirring continuously until thickened.
4. Stir in the shredded Cheddar, a cup at a time, until smooth and creamy.
5. Add the Half & Half or milk, reduce heat to low and heat 5-10 minutes (DO NOT BOIL). Taste and adjust seasonings, remove bay leaf and serve ♥

> **Serving Suggestion:** Garnish Cheddar Broccoli simply: a dusting of paprika. A nice, light meal would include a serving of Nutty Brown Rice and a freshly baked Savory Garden Muffin!

Minestrone
4-6 servings

An excellent soup, thick with vegetables and fragrant with savory herbs and spices. Make minestrone year-round; in summer, with fresh herbs and veggies in abundance, and winter, using tomatoes and herbs put up the summer before or purchased at your local grocery. Minestrone is more a type of soup than an exact recipe. Feel free to substitute veggies. Use what is available when you make it, what you especially like, or what you need to use up.

¼ cup small red beans
¼ cup small white beans
¼ tsp. salt   OR 1 (15-oz) can red beans
1 bay leaf   or any kind you want
4 cups water

4 Tbs. olive oil
2 cloves garlic, minced
1 medium onion (red or yellow) chopped
1 stalk celery, sliced
1 medium carrot, halved lengthwise and sliced
¼ tsp. salt

1 small zucchini, sliced ¼" thick
¼ cup seeded and sliced green bell pepper
¼ cup seeded and sliced red bell pepper

¼ cup <u>each</u> chopped green onion & fresh parsley
1 tsp. basil
¼ tsp. <u>each</u> thyme, rosemary and black pepper

continued →

(Minestrone, continued)

3 cups water (if using canned beans)
1 (15-oz) can tomato sauce
1-2 Tbs. tomato paste

★ note: skip step 1 if using canned beans

1. Soak beans in 2 cups water at least 4 hours (or overnight). In a saucepan (2qt.) combine soaked beans, salt, bay leaf, and 4c. water. Bring to a boil, reduce heat to medium, and cook, covered, until beans are soft and tender, about 1 hour. (Add more water as beans cook. You'll want 3 cups of liquid in the pot when beans are done.)
2. In a large, wide pot (4-6qt.) cook garlic in oil until lightly browned. Add onion, celery, carrot, and salt (and bay leaf if using canned beans). Sauté 7 minutes over medium heat. Add zucchini and the green and red peppers and sauté 5 or 6 minutes more, until veggies are tender but not soft. Add remaining veggies, herbs and seasonings and sauté 1 minute more.
3. Add cooked beans and water (or canned beans and 3 cups fresh water) to veggies in pot. Stir in tomato sauce and 1 Tbs. tomato paste.
4. Bring soup to a full rolling boil, stirring often. Reduce heat to low and simmer, covered, for 15 minutes, stirring occasionally.
5. Taste and adjust seasonings. Add a little more water if desired and/or the last tablespoon of tomato paste. Reduce heat to very low and simmer, covered, for 15 minutes more. Remove bay leaf before serving.

Lentil Soup
4-6 servings

Here's our version of the old classic. The secret to making great lentil soup is cooking the lentils a long time. They should be really soft and saucey when you combine them with the veggies.

- 2 cups dry lentils, rinsed
- ½ tsp. salt
- 2 bay leaves
- 8 cups water

- 2 Tbs. butter or vegetable oil
- 1-2 cloves garlic, minced
- 1 medium onion, chopped
- 2 stalks celery, sliced
- 2 carrots, halved lengthwise and sliced
- ½ tsp. salt

- ½ cup chopped fresh parsley
- ½ tsp. marjoram
- ½ tsp. thyme
- 1 tsp. black pepper

- ¼ cup tomato paste
- 2 Tbs. red wine vinegar
- 1-2 cups water

1. In a large soup pot (4-6 qt.) combine lentils, salt, bay leaves and 8 cups water. Cook, covered, over medium heat until lentils are soft and saucey, 2-3 hours. (Add more

continued →

(Lentil Soup, continued)

water as the lentils cook. You'll want the consistency of a thick, saucey soup when the lentils are done.)

2. In a large, wide pot or frying pan, cook garlic in butter or oil until lightly browned. Add onions, celery, carrots and salt. Sauté 10-12 minutes over medium heat, until tender, stirring often. Stir in parsley, herbs, and seasonings and cook 1-2 minutes.
3. Add veggies to cooked lentils in pot. Stir together.
4. In a small bowl, combine tomato paste and red wine vinegar. Stir into soup. Add more water if soup is too thick.
5. Cook, over medium heat until soup is hot and steaming, stirring often. Reduce heat to low and simmer, covered, for 30 minutes, stirring occasionally.
6. Adjust seasonings to suit your taste. Add a little more water, if necessary; lentils are thirsty things! When satisfied, reduce heat to very low and simmer, covered, until ready to serve. Remove bay leaves before serving.

> Serving Suggestion: Nice garnishes are fresh parsley sprigs with a dollop of yogurt or shredded Swiss or Cheddar cheese. A satisfying meal would include: Lentil soup, Nutty Brown Rice salad, a chunk of cheese and a warm Bran muffin!

U.S. Senate Bean
(White Bean and Ham)
4-6 servings

My Father sent the original recipe clipped from a newspaper. The article claimed it was the same soup served in the Senate dining room. Of course, it's gone through the "Café changes" and come out a much better soup, in my opinion. (Is nothing sacred?!)

1 cup dry small white beans
¼ tsp. salt
6 cups water
¼ cup minced ham
2 bay leaves

2 Tbs. butter or oil
1 clove garlic, minced
1 medium onion, chopped
2 stalks celery, sliced
2 carrots, halved lengthwise and sliced
¼ tsp. salt

¼ cup chopped fresh parsley
¼ cup sliced green onions
½ tsp. black pepper
¼ tsp. marjoram

2 cups peeled and chopped potatoes

2 cups homemade chicken broth
   or 1 (14-oz) can chicken broth

continued →

(U.S. Senate Bean, continued)

1. Soak beans in 3 cups water at least 4 hours (or overnight). Drain. In a saucepan (3 qt.) combine soaked beans, salt, bay leaves, ¼ cup minced ham, and 6 cups water. Bring to a boil, reduce heat to medium and cook, covered, until beans are soft and tender, about 1 hour. (Add more water as the beans cook. You'll want about 4 cups of liquid in the pot when beans are done.)
2. In a large, wide pot (6 qt.) cook garlic in butter or oil until lightly browned. Add onion, celery, carrot, and salt. Sauté 10-12 minutes over medium heat, stirring often until veggies are tender. Stir in parsley, green onions, and seasonings and cook 1-2 minutes longer.
3. In a small saucepan (2 qt.) cover the chopped potatoes with water and cook until tender. Drain, reserving water for later, if needed. Mash potatoes with a fork or wire whisk and set aside.
4. Add beans (and water they cooked in) to veggies in pot. Stir in chicken broth and mashed potatoes. Add reserved potato water if soup is too thick.
5. Bring to a healthy boil over high heat, stirring often. Reduce heat to low and simmer, covered, for 30 minutes, stirring occasionally.
6. Taste and adjust seasonings. To thicken, puree some of the soup and stir back in or simmer uncovered for awhile. Reduce heat to very low and simmer, covered, until ready to serve. Remove bay leaves before serving.

> **serving suggestion:** Old fashioned and comforting, it makes a nice
> ★★★ filling meal with Garden Veggie Pasta & Cornbread

Tomato Tortellini
4-6 servings

An elegant Italian soup that is surprisingly easy to prepare.

2 Tbs. olive oil
1-2 cloves garlic, minced
1 medium onion, chopped
1 stalk celery, sliced
1 small green bell pepper, seeded and chopped
1 small zucchini, halved lengthwise and sliced
½ cup sliced fresh mushrooms
¼ cup grated carrots
¼ tsp. salt

¼ c. chopped parsley
¼ tsp. thyme
¼ tsp. basil
¼ tsp. marjoram
¼ tsp. black pepper

Garnish with Parmesan — Bravo!

3 cups (24-oz) tomato sauce
2 cups water
2 Tbs. tomato paste

4 cups water
¼ tsp. salt
1 cup (4-oz) tortellini

continued →

(Tomato Tortellini, continued)

1. In a large, wide pot, cook garlic in oil until lightly browned. Add remaining veggies and salt; sauté 10-12 minutes over medium heat. Stir in parsley, herbs, and seasonings; cook 1-2 minutes. (Veggies will be tender when done.)
2. Stir in tomato sauce, paste, and 2 cups water. Simmer, covered, over low heat for 15 minutes.
3. In a medium sauce pan bring 4 cups water to a boil. Add tortellini and ¼ tsp. salt, boil again, and cook, uncovered, for 5 minutes. Drain. (Tortellini will be firm when done. They'll soften more in the soup.)
4. Add tortellini to the soup. If soup is too thick, add a little water. Taste, and adjust seasonings. Reduce heat to very low and heat, covered, until ready to serve.

Serving Suggestion: Tomato Tortellini makes a nice, light main-course when served with a fresh green salad and some crusty bread.

Tortellini are small circles of pasta, stuffed with a meat or cheese filling and folded together to form a curious little winged dumpling of sorts. We affectionately refer to them as "bellybuttons" at the Café. You may use whatever variety you prefer. At local grocery stores I've found dried or fresh cheese-filled tortellini. They come in green (spinach) or white (egg) pasta. The fresh taste better than the dried.

Old-Fashioned Turkey Barley
4-6 servings

Old-fashioned and delicious, this is a variation of the soup my mother, Agnes O'Shea, makes every Thanksgiving Friday. My version calls for turkey breast you can buy at the store - if you don't happen to have a turkey carcass to pick over.

    2 Tbs. butter or vegetable oil
    1 medium onion, chopped
    ½ tsp. salt

    ⅓ cup raw barley
    2 stalks celery, sliced
    1 carrot, halved lengthwise and sliced
    ½ cup sliced fresh mushrooms
    1 medium potato, chopped (peeled or not - your choice)
    1 bay leaf

    ½ cup chopped fresh parsley
    ½ cup sliced green onions
    1 tsp. tarragon
    ⅛ tsp. rosemary
    ½ tsp. black pepper

    7 cups homemade chicken broth
        or 4 (14-oz) cans natural chicken broth
    1½ cups (½ lb) cooked turkey breast, cubed

1. In a large, wide pot sauté onions and salt in melted butter or oil for 3-5 minutes over medium-high heat. (Onions should begin to brown.)

Continued →

(Turkey Barley, continued)

2. Add barley, carrots, celery, potato, and bay leaf. Cook, covered, over medium heat for 10 minutes. Stir often.
3. Add remaining veggies, herbs, and black pepper and cook 3-5 minutes more. (Veggies should be tender and barley still a little chewy when done.)
4. Stir in chicken broth, bring to a boil over high heat; reduce heat to medium and simmer, covered, for 15 minutes. Stir occasionally.
5. Add turkey breast, reduce heat to low, and gently simmer 15 minutes. Taste and adjust seasonings. Continue to gently simmer until ready to serve. Remove bay leaf.

> **Serving Suggestion:** Very good served with San Francisco Rice or Garden Veggie Pasta. Add some thinly-sliced toasted Irish Soda Bread and ENJOY!

🍎 Tarragon, affectionately known as "little dragon" because of its coiled roots, is an aromatic anise-flavored herb, delicious with poultry, seafood, vegetables, and eggs. Like any herb, tarragon's flavor diminishes with drying, so use fresh if available. If you grow your own, make sure it's French tarragon, not the hardier but less flavorful Russian tarragon. French tarragon rarely produces fertile flowers so purchase a plant, or better yet, get a cutting from a friend's plant. Preserve some fresh sprigs in a jar of wine vinegar; the tarragon can be removed and used in cooking after flavoring the vinegar for salad dressings. Tarragon overwinters safely in a mild climate if mulched with leaves or grass clippings in the fall, or pot it up and place in a sunny kitchen window to have fresh tarragon all winter long.

Mexi-Corn Chowder
4-6 servings

Cook up a pot any time of the year, hot, cold or mild weather. It's warm, spicy, and satisfying like chili - without beans - so it's lighter and fresher in taste and texture.

4 Tbs. vegetable oil
1-2 cloves garlic
1 medium onion, chopped
1 stalk celery, sliced
1 carrot, chopped
1 green pepper, seeded and chopped
1 red pepper, seeded and chopped
1 jalapeño pepper, seeded and chopped
½ tsp. salt

¼ cup thinly-sliced green onions
¼ cup chopped fresh parsley
¼ cup chopped fresh cilantro, optional
2 cups fresh or frozen corn
2 tsp chili powder
2 tsp. cumin
½ tsp. oregano
½ tsp. black pepper
⅛ tsp. cayenne
1 or 2 dashes Tabasco Sauce

1 (15-oz) can tomato sauce
1 (15-oz.) can crushed peeled tomatoes in puree
2 cups water
2 Tbs. tomato paste

continued ⟶

(Mexi-Corn Chowder, continued)

1. In a large, wide pot (6 qt.), cook garlic in oil until lightly browned. Add onions, celery, carrot, peppers, and salt, and sauté 12 minutes over medium heat, stirring often. Add remaining veggies and spices and cook until carrots and celery are tender, 8-10 minutes. (Stir often as spices have a tendency to stick. Reduce heat to medium-low and/or add a little more vegetable oil if necessary. Sautéing the spices helps develop their flavor.)

2. Stir in tomato sauce, crushed peeled tomatoes, water, and tomato paste. Bring to a boil over high heat, stirring often. Reduce heat to low and simmer, covered, for 30 minutes, stirring occasionally. Add water, if necessary, to thin soup. Taste and adjust seasonings. Reduce heat to very low and gently simmer, covered, until ready to serve.

> Serving Suggestion: Garnish with thinly-sliced green onions or sprigs of fresh parsley and cilantro. Serve with Chicken Couscous or Mexi-Cali Rice and warm Cornbread.

Notes

Potato Cheddar
4-6 servings

This is comfort food at its most comfortable best. It's sure to satisfy and soothe. Add the Cheddar chunks a few minutes before serving— you want the cheese to be melting and chewy but not dissolved when eaten.

  2 lbs. potatoes, peeled and chopped
  water to cover

  2 Tbs. butter or vegetable oil
  1 medium onion, chopped
  1 stalk celery, sliced
  1 carrot, halved lengthwise and sliced
  1 tsp. salt

  ½ cup finely-chopped parsley
  ½ tsp. basil
  ¼ tsp. white pepper

  1 cup "reserved" potato water
  1 tsp. cornstarch
  ¼ cup. cold water

  4 cups milk
  1 cup (4 oz.) Cheddar cheese
          cut into ½" chunks

continued ⟶

(Potato Cheddar, continued)

1. Boil potatoes in a medium pot (3-4 qt.) until soft. Drain, reserving 1 cup of the potato water. Mash half of the potatoes with a fork or wire whisk; leave the other half in chunks. Set aside.
2. In a large, wide pot, heat butter or oil. Sauté onion, carrot, celery, and salt over medium heat for 10-12 minutes. Stir in parsley, basil, and white pepper and cook 1-2 minutes. (Veggies will be tender when done.)
3. Add cooked potato chunks and reserved potato water to veggies. Cook over medium heat until warm. Stir cornstarch into cold water and add, all at once, to the veggie mixture, stirring continuously until thickened. Stir in mashed potatoes.
4. Slowly stir in milk. Heat until hot. (DO NOT BOIL.) Reduce heat to low and stir in Cheddar chunks. Wait 5-10 minutes (for cheese to melt a little).

Serving Suggestion: This soup is great with any vinaigrette-dressed salad, pasta or greens. Serve with warm Bran muffins ♥ A garnish of shredded Cheddar for the soup is nice.

Santa Fe Cheddar
4-6 servings

This suprising soup is smooth and rich with a nice spicy bite. The somewhat unusual marriage of tart apples, jalapeños and Cheddar cheese succeeds deliciously! Adapted from a recipe brought in by one of my crew (clipped from some magazine), it's so good I want to share it with you.

2 Tbs. butter or vegetable oil
1-2 cloves garlic, minced
1 medium onion, chopped
1 large carrot, halved lengthwise and sliced
1 granny Smith apple, peeled, cored, and chopped
2 jalapeño peppers, seeded and minced
¼ cup _each_ sliced green and red bell pepper
¼ tsp. salt

2 Tbs. _each_ minced fresh cilantro and parsley
1 small tomato, seeded and chopped
½ cup finely-sliced green onions
¼ tsp. white pepper
1 bay leaf

⅔ cup flour
1 Tbs. cornstarch
3½ cups homemade chicken broth
   or 2 (14-oz) cans chicken broth
⅓ cup white wine, optional
4 cups (1 lb.) shredded Cheddar cheese
2 cups Half & Half or milk

continued ⟶

(Santa Fe Cheddar, continued)

1. In a large, wide pot cook garlic in oil or butter until lightly browned. Add onion, carrot, apple, peppers, and salt; Sauté 7 minutes over medium heat. Add remaining veggies, white pepper, and bay leaf; sauté 5-7 minutes more. (Veggies and apple will be tender when done.)
2. In a small bowl stir together flour and cornstarch. To the soup pot with the veggies add 1/2 of the chicken broth. Cook over medium heat until hot but not boiling and stir in the flour/cornstarch mixture, a little at a time, until all has been added and the veggie mixture is bubbly and thick.
3. Add the remaining chicken broth, a little at a time, stirring continuously until thickened.
4. Add optional white wine, if desired. Stir in the shredded Cheddar, a cup at a time, until smooth.
5. Add Half & Half or milk, reduce heat to low and heat 5-10 minutes. (DO NOT BOIL.) Taste and adjust seasonings, remove bay leaf, and serve. ★

Serving Suggestion: Garnish with a few choice parsley or cilantro sprigs. This soup goes well with many salads. Try Mexi-cali Rice, fresh Tomato Parmesan, and/or Chicken Szechuan. Round it off with a Mexican Corn Muffin. Enjoy!

"Summer cooking implies
a sense of immediacy,
a capacity to capture
the essence
of the fleeting moment."

Elizabeth David

Salads

- ▲ An Introduction 64
- ▲ How To Cook Pasta Perfectly For Salads 68
- ▲ A Few Things About Teriyaki Chicken 70

- ▲ Pesto Pasta 73
- ▲ Antipasto Pasta 74
- ▲ Spinach Chicken Pasta 76
- ▲ Thai Chicken Pasta 78
- ▲ Turkey Pasta Mayo 80
- ▲ Turkey Tortellini 82
- ▲ Ricotta Tortellini 84
- ▲ Oriental Sesame Pasta 85
- ▲ Chicken Szechuan 86
- ▲ Garden Veggie Pasta 88
- ▲ Pasta á la greek 89

- ▲ Fresh Tomato Parmesan Pasta 90
- ▲ Oregon Shrimp Pasta 91
- ▲ Albacore Tuna Pasta 92
- ▲ Quick Hummus 93
- ▲ Chicken Couscous 94
- ▲ Nutty Brown Rice 96
- ▲ Mexi-Cali Rice 98
- ▲ Smoked Turkey Wild Rice 100
- ▲ Sesame Chicken Rice 102
- ▲ San Francisco Rice 104
- ▲ Leslie's Zingy Potato Salad 105

Salads

Our salads show the creative flair of the Café, so we put a lot of thought and energy into them. Many new kinds of "pre-made" salads are available these days that masquerade as fresh. Masquerade, of course, is the key word. <u>Fresh is fresh is fresh</u>. You can't take a salad that's been prepared somewhere in Los Angeles, ship it up north in a freezer truck, store it in a warehouse freezer for who knows how long, then receive it in your kitchen to serve to your precious customers as a healthful, freshly made salad. Not a chance! We'll always make our own.

Salads have really come of age. A frugal food, many of the recipes included here have very inexpensive ingredients but give the feeling of abundance and comfort. Light, fresh, and healthful with all the interesting grains, pastas, and colorful vegetables in them, they nourish body a<u>nd</u> mind. And, if you are watching your fat intake, they can be made very low in fat.

No longer do we have to settle for an iceberg lettuce salad with a few grated carrots, a limp cucumber slice, and a hard, tasteless wedge of winter tomato. Praise fresh food and the incredible variety of salad fixings available today! What a pleasure to discover uses for all the great and unusual ingredients. Next time you go to the grocery store take a look around the produce section. It's an eye-opening experience!

If you are a gardener, as I am, this awareness takes on a new dimension. You can grow your own vegetables, herbs, and even flowers for salad making.

continued →

I grow many of the vegetables and herbs for the Café's summer menu and get great pleasure from it. If you aren't a gardener but desire fresh fruit, vegetables, and more, grown in the very soil you call home, then the Corvallis Farmers' Market is for you! A very well-organized and friendly group, they offer an abundance of fresh produce every Wednesday and Saturday from May through November. Check it out – it's fantastic!

    All of the salads in this book are composed of pasta, rice, or grains with many vegetables, cheeses, seafoods, and meats. Much of our food is vegetarian, including the salads, but if you find a salad to make that includes meat (and you don't), just leave the meat out. Our salads have enough other ingredients to be delicious "sans carné." (Some would say they're even better!)

    These salads are quick to make, keep for several days, and can be served at room temperature, chilled, or heated in the microwave. Please read "How to cook pasta perfectly" (p.68) before making any of the pasta salads; it contains important information. I hope these salads become favorites of yours.

> Serving temperature: Many salads taste better after resting an hour. Those with an oil-based dressing and which don't contain meats, fish, or mayonaisse can remain in a cool place while flavor develops; others should be refrigerated. Salads taste best at room temperature or slightly chilled, not icy-cold. Take from the refrigerator a little while
>
> continued →

before serving so they have time to reach the proper temperature.

Presentation: Salads are a thing of beauty. Serve on a large leaf of lettuce, spinach, or kale arranged on a pretty glass plate. Save a few especially nice ingredients for a garnish. Serve with freshly baked bread or muffins (or reheat some from your last batch). An extra-nice touch is an edible flower such as a nasturtium or marigold, or a sprig of fresh rosemary or mint.

Portions: These are hard to gauge. At the Café we serve large 12 oz. servings. Some people prefer more, some less. Also take into account whether it's the main-course or a side serving. The stated number of servings a recipe makes are main-course servings. Figure on 2-3 side servings per main-course serving. Don't worry if you've made more than you need, it keeps well and will make an excellent meal the next day.

Storing: Refrigerate left-over salad in a tightly covered container. Most of the salads will keep for 2 or 3 days, actually improving as the flavors blend and mellow. You may find that your salad is a little dry the next day. The pasta has a tendency to soak up the dressing as it sits. Moisten with a little more vinaigrette or mayonnaise.

continued ⟶

note ♥ Fresh Herbs Vs. Dried Herbs

I used the figures for dried herbs in these recipes because they are so readily available, BUT, if you grow or have a source for fresh herbs by all means use them. Dried herbs are fine, but fresh herbs are wonderful! They are interchangeable but the amount must be converted. It's easy! When using fresh, use 3 times the amount of dried herb called for in the recipe.

example: ½ tsp. basil = 1½ tsp. fresh basil

....

Ideas ♥

How To Cook Pasta Perfectly for Salads

½ lb. pasta (about 4 cups)
16 cups (1 gallon) water
2 tsp. salt

1. In a very large pot, bring water to a full rolling boil. Add salt.

2. Add pasta all at once, stirring hard to prevent it from sticking to the bottom of the pan or to itself.

3. Start timing when the water returns to a full boil. Generally pasta needs about 8-10 minutes to cook "al dente" (firm to the bite). During the cooking time, stir occasionally to keep pasta moving and separate. After 8 minutes, check to see if it's done by removing a piece, cooling it a little, and biting in. It will be firm (but not hard) in the middle when done. <u>Do Not Overcook</u>. Overcooked pasta is too mushy for a good pasta salad. It's better to throw it away and start again.

4. Pour the pasta, water and all, into a large colander and drain well. (Warning! Rising steam!) Immediately drench with cool water. Keep rinsing and moving the pasta around (for even cooling), until the pasta is cool. Drain, shake off excess water, and pat dry with a clean towel. Now you're ready to complete your delicious salad!

continued ⟶

(How To Cook Pasta, continued)

5. Pasta for salads can be prepared the night before, covered with the vinaigrette dressing, and left to marinate overnight in the refrigerator. This makes a most excellent salad! When you complete the salad the next day, you may find you need to add more vinaigrette dressing since the pasta will have soaked up what was placed on it the night before. It's perfectly fine to add more dressing!

For A Mayonnaise-Dressed Pasta Salad

The above step (#5) is a necessity. You must add all the vinaigrette dressing the recipe calls for, refrigerate and let marinate overnight. The next day you will complete the salad, adding the veggies and/or meats and cheeses, and the mayonnaise. Notice how well the mayonnaise coats the pasta! Do not add more vinaigrette dressing at this point as it would cause the mayonnaise to separate.

types of Pasta used here: tortellini, mostaccioli, rotini or spiral, bow-tie, shell

A few things about Teriyaki Chicken

Bok Bok!

How to soak it:

Rinse skinless boneless breast of chicken in lots of cold water. Drain and pat dry. Place in a plastic, glass, or stainless steel pan large enough so that the chicken is not crowded. Cover with Teriyaki sauce (p.33) stirring a little to surround the chicken completely. Cover and place in the refrigerator for 4 to 8 hours.

♥ note: The longer chicken (or anything else you marinate) is left in the teriyaki sauce, the more flavor it absorbs. Small pieces require less marinating than larger ones. Food will marinate twice as fast at room temperature than if it is marinated in the refrigerator.

Remove marinated chicken from the refrigerator and take a peek. The chicken should be stained a rich brown. If one side is lighter, push it more deeply into the teriyaki (or turn it over) and soak a little longer. When the chicken is an even rich medium brown color, it's ready.

How to cook it:

Transfer the chicken and teriyaki sauce into a stainless steel pot. Bring to a boil, reduce heat, and simmer over low heat until chicken is firm to the touch, 15 to 20 minutes. Do not boil rapidly, or the chicken will be tough. Another test: Cut into the largest piece. It should be cooked throughout.

continued →

(Teriyaki Chicken, continued)

(How to cook, continued)
When the chicken is done, remove from the pot and set aside to cool slightly. Then cut into bite-sized pieces and use in whatever wonderful dish you want to create. If desired, add a little of the cooked teriyaki sauce to your salad - it enriches the flavor. But I don't recommend using it to marinate chicken again. It's done its job and doesn't keep well.

What to use it in:
  Oriental Sesame Pasta (p. 85)
  Thai Chicken Pasta (p. 78)
  Sesame Chicken Rice (p. 102)
  Chicken Szechuan (p. 86)

A word about Barbecue:
Teriyaki Sauce makes an excellent marinade for barbecued chicken. After marinating the meat as directed above, place it on the grill and barbecue as usual, basting with the teriyaki left from marinating.
  <u>WORD OF CAUTION</u>: Do not use the uncooked teriyaki sauce in anything that will not be fully cooked before being served. It could contain bacteria from the raw chicken that soaked in it.

continued ⟶

(Teriyaki Chicken, continued)

(A word about Barbecue, continued)

If you are a Vegetarian and want to enjoy a teriyaki barbecue or if you're just feeling adventurous, I wholeheartedly recommend teriyaki tofu! Use a firm tofu and cut into 1/3-1/2 inch thick slices. Follow directions for chicken but only soak for 3-4 hours. Delicious!

Another idea: A teriyaki chicken kabob! Marinate chunks of chicken and place on a metal skewer alternating with chunks of fresh pineapple, onion, green and red pepper, whole mushrooms, and thin slices of fresh ginger. Baste with leftover teriyaki sauce.

> hint: When cooking teriyaki chicken always make more chicken than you'll need. Some of the recipes call for such a small amount of teriyaki chicken that you may choose to make something else rather than bother... even though what you really wanted... A supply of already prepared teriyaki chicken, squirreled away in the freezer, will solve the dilemma! It will keep for several months, frozen.

Pesto Pasta
3-4 servings

½ lb. rotini pasta (about 4 cups)
½ cup Vinaigrette dressing (p. 25)

½ cup Pesto (p. 32)
½ cup Vinaigrette dressing (p. 25)

¼ cup thinly-sliced red onion
1 small zucchini, quartered lengthwise & sliced
1 small yellow squash, quartered lengthwise & sliced
1 medium tomato, seeded and chopped
½ cup sliced, pitted black olives
1 (2-oz.) jar sliced, roasted pimentos, drained
   or ¼ cup seeded and sliced red bell pepper

1. Cook pasta in lots of boiling, salted water for 8-10 minutes. Drain well. (See p. 68, "How To Cook Pasta Perfectly.")
2. Mix the pasta and Vinaigrette together in a pretty serving bowl. Set aside.
3. In a smaller bowl, mix together pesto and the second ½ cup Vinaigrette. Set aside.
4. Prepare the veggies and add to the serving bowl with pasta. Stir in the pesto and mix well.
5. Cover and let sit, refrigerated or at room temperature, until ready to serve.

> **Serving Suggestion:** Pesto Pasta looks great garnished with fresh basil leaves, parsley sprigs or (if you're *really* inspired) a purple chive flower! Try serving with Garden Vegetable Barley Soup and cornbread.

Antipasto Pasta
4-6 servings

Literally translated, antipasto means "before the pasta." It consists of a dish of appetizers such as cheeses, meats, olives, and marinated vegetables. We combine the two courses in this salad!

6 oz. large (1-inch) shell pasta (about 3 cups)
½ cup Vinaigrette dressing (p. 25)

¼ lb. each: lean ham, turkey breast, salami, and provolone cheese, cut into small pieces.
1 small zucchini, halved lengthwise and sliced
1 small tomato, seeded and chopped
    or ½ cup halved cherry tomatoes
½ cup sliced celery
½ cup thinly-sliced red onion
¼ cup seeded and sliced green bell pepper
¼ cup finely-chopped fresh parsley
¼ cup sliced, pitted black olives
¼ cup whole pimento-stuffed small green olives
1 (4-oz.) jar sliced, roasted pimentos, drained
    or ½ cup seeded and sliced red bell pepper
¼ cup grated Parmesan cheese
2 Tbs. red wine vinegar
½ cup Vinaigrette dressing (p. 25)

1. Cook pasta in lots of boiling, salted water for 8-10 minutes. Drain well. (See p. 68, "How to Cook Pasta Perfectly.")

continued →

(Antipasto Pasta, continued)

2. Mix the pasta and vinaigrette together in your nicest serving bowl. Set aside.
3. Prepare the veggies, meats, and cheese and add to serving bowl with pasta. Stir in the Parmesan cheese, red wine vinegar, and remaining ½ cup Vinaigrette. Mix well.
4. Cover and refrigerate until ready to serve. Add a little more Vinaigrette before serving, if desired.

> Serving Suggestion: A main-course salad, Antipasto Pasta needs only a garnish of parsley sprigs, a side of a favorite steamed vegetable (asparagus in season!), and some crusty bread to satisfy completely! This is a great pot-luck salad! Double the recipe for your next get-together.

notes ❀

Spinach Chicken Pasta
4-6 servings

1 lb. large (1-inch) shell pasta (about 8 cups)
1/4 cup Vinaigrette dressing (p.25)

1/2 lb. boneless, skinless chicken breast (about 2 chicken breast halves)
1/4 cup thinly-sliced red onion
1 small tomato, seeded and chopped

Dressing:
1 cup spinach leaves, washed, dried and packed
2 Tbs. chopped parsley
2 Tbs. sliced scallions
1 small clove garlic, minced
2 tsp. fresh lemon juice
2 tsp. Dijon mustard
1/4 tsp. salt
1/8 tsp. black pepper
1/2 tsp. dill weed
1/4 cup mayonnaise
1/2 cup buttermilk

1. Cook pasta in lots of boiling, salted water for 8-10 minutes. Drain well. (See p.68, "How To Cook Pasta Perfectly.")
2. Mix the pasta and Vinaigrette together in a nice serving bowl. Set aside.
3. Heat 3 to 4 cups water to a low simmer. Add salt and chicken; simmer slowly in a covered pot until chicken is firm to the touch, 15-20 minutes.

continued ⟶

(Spinach-Chicken Pasta, continued)

4. Remove chicken from pan. (Refrigerate or freeze broth for other uses.) Cool chicken slightly and chop into bite-sized pieces. Add to pasta.
5. Prepare red onion and tomato. Combine with chicken and pasta.
6. Prepare dressing ingredients. Combine in a blender or food processor; blend until smooth. Pour over salad and stir well.
7. Cover and refrigerate until ready to serve.

> Serving Suggestion: Serve Spinach-Chicken Pasta on a bed of fresh spinach leaves with some sliced ripe tomatoes for a refreshing low calorie meal. Great on a warm summer evening.

....
Notes ✶

Thai Chicken Pasta
4-6 servings

This salad contains Teriyaki chicken which must be marinated 4-8 hours before cooking. (See p.70, "A few things about Teriyaki Chicken.")

6 oz. bow-tie pasta (about 3 cups)
1 lb. Teriyaki chicken (p.70), cut into strips
    (about 4 chicken breast halves)
½ cup julienne red bell pepper
½ cup julienne green bell pepper
½ cup julienne carrot
1 cup separated broccoli florets
¼ cup thinly-sliced green onions
¼ cup finely-chopped fresh parsley
¼ cup finely-chopped fresh cilantro
½ cup fresh or frozen pea pods

Dressing:
½ cup vegetable oil (peanut oil is nice here)
½ cup peanut butter
3 Tbs. fresh lemon juice
3 Tbs. soy sauce
1 Tbs. hot chili oil or ¼ tsp. cayenne pepper
1 clove garlic, minced
1 Tbs. grated fresh ginger
1 jalapeño pepper, seeded and minced.
1 Tbs. brown sugar
½ tsp. black or white pepper

continued ⟶

(Thai Chicken Pasta, continued)

1. Cook pasta in lots of boiling, salted water for 8-10 minutes. Drain well. (See p. 68, "How To Cook Pasta Perfectly.") Place pasta in pretty serving bowl.
2. Prepare chicken and veggies and add to pasta.
3. Prepare dressing ingredients. Combine in a blender or food processor; blend until smooth. Pour over salad and stir well.
4. Cover and refrigerate until ready to serve.

> **Serving Suggestion:**  Garnish with chopped peanuts and a few sprigs of cilantro. Thai Chicken Pasta is delicious served warm! Microwave a minute or two, until hot, or heat, covered, in a conventional oven. Heating heightens aroma & flavor.

Jalapeño peppers must be handled very carefully. It's best either to wear protective gloves or to avoid touching the seeds or the white vein inside. That's where capsicin, a severe skin irritant, lurks. If you do burn yourself, milk, vinegar, or fat applied to the burn may help ease the pain. Make you wonder why we eat them? Other than the fact that they taste so good, they are also a good source of vitamin A and, in fresh peppers, Vitamin C. People in hot climates experience a sort of natural air-conditioning when they ingest hot peppers - they perspire! Also, there is a lower incidence of stomach cancer in cultures that make hot peppers a staple.

Turkey Pasta Mayo
2-4 Servings

Early morning or night before:

    1/2 lb. large (1 inch) shell pasta (about 4 cups)
    1/4 cup Vinaigrette dressing (p. 25)
    ♥ note: Pasta and Vinaigrette dressing must be combined at least 8 hours before completing salad. (See p. 68, "How To Cook Pasta Perfectly"..."For A Mayonnaise Dressed Salad.")

Later:

    1/2 lb. cooked turkey breast, cubed
    1/2 cup sliced celery
    1/2 cup peeled, seeded, and chopped cucumber
    1/4 cup thinly-sliced green onions
    1/4 cup finely-chopped fresh parsley
    1 cup mayonnaise
    salt and black pepper, to taste

1. At least 8 hours before completing salad, cook pasta in lots of boiling, salted water for 8-10 minutes. Drain well. (See p. 68-69, "How To Cook Pasta Perfectly"... For A Mayonnaise Dressed Salad.") Mix the pasta and Vinaigrette dressing and refrigerate, covered, for at least 8 hours.
2. Remove pasta from refrigerator. Place in a pretty serving bowl and set aside.

                                          continued ⟶

(Turkey Pasta Mayo, continued)

3. Prepare turkey and veggies and add to pasta. Stir in mayonnaise and blend well. Add salt and pepper to taste.
4. Cover and refrigerate until ready to serve. Add a little more mayonnaise, if desired.

Serving Suggestion: This salad looks cool and refreshing garnished with sliced green onions or fresh parsley sprigs and served on a bed of fresh leaf lettuce.
 A delicious meal would be: Turkey Pasta Mayo Salad, Old fashioned Turkey Barley Soup, and Irish Soda bread. Lots of turkey, I know, but they are *so* good together.

notes

Turkey Tortellini
3-4 servings

Early in the morning or night before:

9 oz. turkey & cheese filled tortellini (2½-3 cups)
¼ c. Vinaigrette dressing (p. 25)
♥note: the tortellini and Vinaigrette dressing must be combined at least 8 hours before completing Salad. (See p. 68, "How To Cook Pasta Perfectly"..."For A Mayonnaise Dressed Salad.")

Later:
¼ cup seeded and sliced green bell pepper
1 (2-oz.) jar sliced, roasted pimento, drained
   or ¼ cup seeded and sliced red bell pepper
½ cup sliced, pitted black olives
1 small zucchini, quartered lengthwise and sliced
½ cup thinly-sliced red onion
1 medium tomato, seeded and chopped
¼ cup finely-chopped fresh parsley
1 cup mayonnaise
salt and black pepper, to taste

1. At least 8 hours before completing Salad, cook tortellini in lots of boiling, salted water for 7 minutes. Drain; rinse with plenty of cold water, drain again, and pat dry. Mix the tortellini and Vinaigrette dressing and refrigerate, covered, for at least 8 hours. (See p. 69, "For A Mayonnaise Dressed Salad.")

continued →

(Turkey Tortellini, continued)

2. Remove tortellini from refrigerator. Place in a pretty serving bowl and set aside.
3. Prepare veggies and add to the tortellini. Stir in mayonnaise and blend well. Add salt and pepper to taste.
4. Cover and refrigerate until ready to serve. Add a little more mayonnaise, if desired.

> Variations: Mayonnaise not in your diet plan? Make this salad with a Vinaigrette dressing. Just follow the instructions for Ricotta Tortellini.

Notes:

Ricotta Tortellini
3-4 servings

9 oz. cheese-filled tortellini (2½-3 cups) 🍎
½ cup Vinaigrette dressing (p. 25)

¼ cup thinly-sliced green onions
½ cup julienne carrots
¼ cup julienne celery
1 cup separated broccoli florets
1 (2-oz) jar sliced pimentos, drained
   or ¼ cup seeded and sliced red bell pepper
1 medium tomato, seeded and chopped
¼ cup finely-chopped fresh parsley
2 Tbs. grated Parmesan cheese
¼ cup Vinaigrette dressing (p. 25)

1. Cook tortellini in plenty of boiling, salted water for 7 minutes. Drain, rinse with lots of cold water, drain again, and pat dry.
2. Mix the tortellini and ½ c. Vinaigrette dressing together in a nice serving bowl. Set aside.
3. Prepare the veggies and add to the serving bowl with pasta. Stir in the Parmesan cheese and remaining Vinaigrette dressing; mix well.
4. Cover and let sit, refrigerated or at room temperature, until ready to serve. Add more Vinaigrette, if desired.

🍎 You can buy dried and fresh cheese-filled tortellini at local groceries. Buy fresh whenever you can—they taste better!

Oriental Sesame Pasta
2-4 servings

6 oz. bow-tie pasta (about 3 cups)
½ cup Oriental dressing (p. 28)

¼ cup sesame seeds
1 Tbs. sesame oil

¾ cup separated broccoli florets
½ cup julienne celery
½ cup julienne carrots
½ cup julienne zucchini
¼ cup thinly-sliced green onion
¼ cup finely-chopped parsley
½ cup sliced water chestnuts
1 (5½-oz) jar baby sweet corn, drained
½ cup fresh or frozen pea pods
¼-½ cup Oriental dressing (p. 28)

> **Variation**
> Add a cup of teriyaki chicken or fresh bay shrimp to this recipe. Tasty!

1. Cook pasta in lots of boiling, salted water for 8-10 minutes. Drain well. (See p. 68, "How To Cook Pasta Perfectly.")
2. Mix pasta and Oriental dressing together in a pretty bowl. Set aside.
3. In a frying pan, toast sesame seeds in oil until golden brown. Set aside to cool.
4. Prepare veggies and add to bowl with pasta. Stir in sesame seeds and remaining dressing. Mix well.
5. Cover and let sit, refrigerated or at room temperature, until ready to serve. You can add a little more dressing, if desired.

Chicken Szechuan
2-4 Servings

This salad contains Teriyaki chicken which must be marinated 4-8 hours before cooking. (See "A few things about Teriyaki chicken," p. 70.)

Tina Chow created this salad. Tina worked at the Café a few years ago and contributed, along with her good energy, several of our all-time-favorite salads.

   ½ lb. small spiral pasta (about 3½ cups)
   ½ cup Oriental dressing (p.28)

   1 cup chopped Teriyaki chicken (p.70)
      (about 1 chicken breast half)
   ½ cup fresh or frozen julienne pea pods
   ½ cup julienne carrots
   ½ cup sliced water chestnuts
   ¼ cup thinly-sliced green onions
   ¼ cup finely-chopped fresh parsley or cilantro
   1 (5½-oz) jar Baby Sweet Corn, drained
   ½ cup Oriental dressing (p.28)

1. Cook pasta in lots of boiling, salted water for 8-10 minutes. Drain well. (See p. 68, "How To Cook Pasta Perfectly.")
2. Mix the pasta and ½ cup Oriental dressing together in a pretty serving bowl. Set aside.
3. Prepare chicken and veggies and add to the serving bowl with pasta. Stir in the remaining ½ cup Oriental dressing and mix well.

continued ⟶

(Chicken Szechuan, continued)

4. Cover and refrigerate until ready to serve. Add more Oriental dressing, if desired.

Serving Suggestion: Chicken Szechuan makes a fantastic presentation on a bed of red chard leaves garnished with 2 or 3 Baby Sweet Corn ears and some julienne green onions strewn over it.

For a hearty meal, serve with a steaming bowl of Lentil soup and cornbread.

Cilantro, also called Chinese parsley, is the leaf of the herb coriander. It has a distinctive fresh, pungent flavor and is excellent in Oriental and Mexican cuisine. (Salsa just isn't the same without it!) Very popular now, it can be found in the produce section of most groceries. Store by standing the cilantro bunch stems down in a glass of water, covered with a plastic bag, in the refrigerator. It will last several days.

. . . .

notes ♥

Garden Veggie Pasta
2-4 servings

½ lb. rainbow rotini (about 4 cups)
½ cup Vinaigrette dressing (p. 25)

1 small zucchini, halved lengthwise and sliced
1 small carrot, halved lengthwise and sliced
½ cup separated broccoli florets
¼ cup sliced celery
¼ cup seeded and sliced cucumber
¼ cup seeded and sliced green pepper
1 (2-oz) jar sliced, roasted pimentos, drained
   or ¼ cup seeded and sliced red bell pepper
¼ cup thinly-sliced green onions
¼ cup finely-chopped fresh parsley
½ cup sliced, pitted black olives
¼ - ½ cup Vinaigrette dressing (p. 25)

1. Cook pasta in lots of boiling, salted water for 8-10 minutes. Drain well. (See p. 68, "How To Cook Pasta Perfectly.")
2. Mix pasta and vinaigrette together in your favorite serving bowl. Set aside.
3. Prepare the veggies and add to the bowl with pasta. Stir in remaining dressing. Mix well.
4. Cover and let sit, refrigerated or at room temperature, until ready to serve. Add a little more dressing, if desired.

 Rainbow rotini is spiral shaped pasta made from semolina dough that has been colored with vegetables; purple from beets, orange from tomatoes, and green from spinach. Your kids will love this salad!

Pasta á la Greek
4-6 servings

½ lb. mostaccioli pasta (about 4 cups)
½ cup Vinaigrette dressing (p. 25)

¼ lb. feta cheese, chopped into bite-sized pieces.
½ cup julienne zucchini
½ cup thinly-sliced red onion
1 small tomato, seeded and sliced
¼ cup finely-chopped fresh parsley
½ cup sliced, pitted black olives
1 (6-oz) jar marinated artichoke hearts
  (slice artichokes and add marinade, too)
1 (2-oz) jar sliced, roasted pimentos, drained.
¼ tsp. <u>each</u> basil, oregano
             salt & black pepper
¼ cup grated Parmesan cheese
¼ - ½ cup Vinaigrette dressing (p. 25)

1. Cook pasta in lots of boiling, salted water for 8-10 minutes. Drain well. (See p. 68 "How To Cook Pasta Perfectly.")
2. Mix pasta and Vinaigrette together in a pretty serving bowl. Set aside.
3. Prepare feta cheese and veggies and add to pasta. Stir in herbs, seasonings, Parmesan cheese and remaining Vinaigrette. Mix well.
4. Cover and let sit, refrigerated or at room temperature, until ready to serve. Add more Vinaigrette, if desired.

Fresh Tomato Parmesan
2-4 servings

A simple salad to make at the height of the growing season when juicy ripe tomatoes and fresh, pungent basil abound.

½ lb. small spiral pasta (about 3½ cups)
½ cup Vinaigrette dressing (p. 25)

2 large ripe tomatoes, seeded and chopped
¼ cup packed fresh basil leaves, thinly-sliced 🍅
2 Tbs. finely-chopped fresh parsley
¼ cup grated Parmesan cheese
1 tsp. fresh lemon juice
¼ tsp. each salt and black pepper, more to taste.
¼ cup olive oil

1. Cook pasta in lots of boiling salted water for 8-10 minutes. Drain well. (See p. 68, "How to Cook Pasta Perfectly.")
2. Mix the pasta and Vinaigrette together in a pretty serving bowl. Set aside.
3. Prepare the veggies and add to the serving bowl with pasta. Stir in Parmesan cheese, lemon juice, seasonings and olive oil. Mix well.
4. Cover and let sit, refrigerated or at room temperature, until ready to serve. Add more Vinaigrette, if desired.

🍅 Basil is called the tomato herb; the two are exquisite together. Some say tomatoes always grow better and are more flavorful with basil planted next to them.

Oregon Shrimp Pasta
2-4 servings

½ lb. bow-tie pasta (about 4 cups)
½ cup Vinaigrette dressing (p. 25)

1½ cups (about ½ lb.) tiny bay shrimp
½ cup sliced celery
½ cup fresh or frozen peas
¼ cup thinly-sliced green onions
¼ cup finely-chopped fresh parsley
½ cup sliced, pitted black olives
1 (2-oz) jar sliced, roasted pimentos
½ tsp. basil
½ tsp. dill weed
2 tsp. Dijon mustard
½ cup Vinaigrette dressing (p.25)
salt & pepper to taste

1. Cook pasta in lots of boiling, salted water 8-10 minutes. Drain well. (See p. 68, "How to Cook Pasta Perfectly.")
2. Mix pasta and Vinaigrette together in a pretty serving bowl. Set aside.
3. Prepare veggies and add to the bowl with pasta. Stir in herbs, mustard, remaining dressing, and seasonings. Mix well.
4. Rinse shrimp under cold water and pat dry with a clean towel. Add to salad; mix well.
5. Cover and refrigerate until ready to serve. Adjust seasonings with salt & pepper and add a little more Vinaigrette, if desired.

Albacore Tuna Pasta
2-4 servings

½ lb. mostaccioli pasta (about 4 cups)
½ cup Vinaigrette dressing (p. 25)

½ cup sliced celery
¼ cup thinly-sliced red onion
¼ cup seeded and sliced green bell pepper
¼ cup finely-chopped fresh parsley
½ cup sliced, pitted black olives
1 (2-oz) jar sliced, roasted pimentos, drained
1 (6-oz) can Albacore tuna, drained
¼ tsp. <u>each</u> salt and black pepper
1 Tbs. red wine vinegar
¼ - ½ cup Vinaigrette dressing

1. Cook pasta in lots of boiling, salted water for 8-10 minutes. Drain well. (See p. 68 "How To Cook Pasta Perfectly.")
2. Mix the pasta and Vinaigrette together in your most "sea-worthy" serving bowl. Set aside.
3. Prepare the veggies and add to pasta. Add the drained tuna, salt and pepper, vinegar and remaining Vinaigrette. Mix well.
4. Cover and refrigerate until ready to serve. Adjust seasonings with salt & pepper and add more Vinaigrette, if desired.

Quick Hummus
1 cup

Now you've added the 1/2 cup garbanzo beans to your Chicken Couscous Salad (p. 94). You stand there looking at the remaining cup of beans in the can. What are you going to do with them? Good question. Here's an idea! Instead of putting them in the refrigerator, where despite your good intentions they have a chance of being forgotten, whip up some Quick Hummus to serve before or with the Chicken Couscous. Accompany with whole-grain crackers, fresh cucumber spears, red bell pepper slices, endive leaves, or pita bread.

- 1 cup cooked garbanzo beans
- 2 Tbs. minced parsley
- 1-2 large cloves garlic
- 3 Tbs. olive oil
- 2 Tbs. fresh lemon juice
- 1/2 tsp. salt
- 1/8 tsp. white pepper
- 1/8 tsp. cayenne

1. Put everything in your blender or food processor. Mix until smooth.
2. Cover and let sit, refrigerated or at room temperature, until ready to serve.

Chicken Couscous
4-6 servings

1 lb. skinless, boneless chicken breast (about 4 chicken breast halves)
½ tsp. salt
4 cups water

¼ cup pine nuts or cashews

Dressing
   ¼ cup fresh lemon juice
   ¼ cup olive oil
   1 clove garlic, finely minced
   ½ tsp. cumin
   ½ tsp. curry
   ¼ tsp. salt
   ¼ tsp. white or black pepper
   ½ - 1½ tsp. Tabasco sauce, to taste

> For related recipe see Quick Hummus p. 93.

1½ cups uncooked couscous
2 cups broth (reserved from cooking chicken)
½ cup julienne red pepper
¼ cup thinly-sliced green onion
¼ cup finely-chopped fresh parsley
1 small tomato, seeded and diced
⅓ cup dried currants
½ cup cooked garbanzo beans, optional

1. In a large pan bring water to a boil. Reduce heat to low; add chicken and salt. Cover and cook, simmering gently, until chicken is firm to the touch and thoroughly cooked, 15-20 minutes. Remove chicken, set aside to cool. Reserve chicken broth.

continued →

(Chicken Couscous, continued)

2. Toast pine nuts or cashews in a 350°F oven 15-20 minutes. Set aside to cool.
3. Combine dressing ingredients in a pretty serving bowl.
4. Cut cooked chicken into bite-sized pieces and stir into dressing in serving bowl. (The chicken will marinate while you prepare the remaining ingredients.)
5. Measure 2 cups of reserved chicken broth and bring to a boil in the pan used to cook the chicken. Stir in couscous, turn off heat, cover immediately, and let sit for 10 minutes. Uncover, fluff with a fork. Cool.
6. Prepare veggies and add to chicken and dressing in serving bowl. Add cooled couscous, dried currants, toasted nuts, and optional garbanzo beans. Stir to mix.
7. Cover and refrigerate until ready to serve.

Variations: Make it meat-free! Just as good without the chicken; we often serve it this way at the Café. Just skip the chicken instructions and substitute water for broth in Step 5.

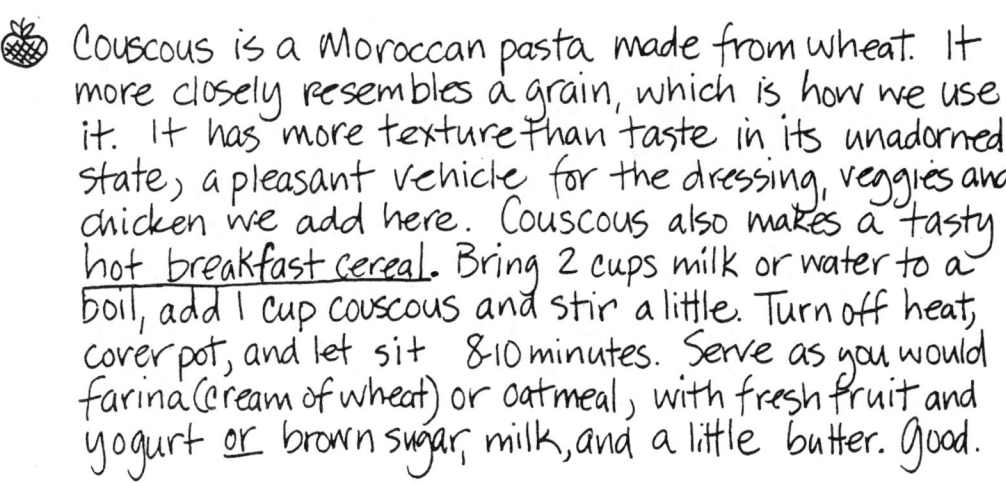

Couscous is a Moroccan pasta made from wheat. It more closely resembles a grain, which is how we use it. It has more texture than taste in its unadorned state, a pleasant vehicle for the dressing, veggies and chicken we add here. Couscous also makes a tasty hot breakfast cereal. Bring 2 cups milk or water to a boil, add 1 cup couscous and stir a little. Turn off heat, cover pot, and let sit 8-10 minutes. Serve as you would farina (cream of wheat) or oatmeal, with fresh fruit and yogurt or brown sugar, milk, and a little butter. Good.

Nutty Brown Rice
2-4 servings

1 Tbs. vegetable oil
1 cup long-grain brown rice
½ tsp. salt
2 cups water

1 cup coarsely chopped walnuts
1 large Granny Smith apple, peeled, cored, and chopped
2 Tbs. fresh lemon juice
1 medium cucumber, peeled, quartered and sliced
½ cup sliced green onions
½ cup seeded and chopped green pepper
¼ cup dried currants

Dressing
   3/4 – 1 cup mayonnaise or unflavored yogurt
   1 Tbs. soy sauce
   1 Tbs. rice vinegar
   ½ tsp. curry powder
   ⅛ tsp. cayenne

1. In a medium saucepan, heat oil. Add rice and stir continuously for 3-4 minutes while the rice toasts. (It will crackle and brown slightly.) Add water and salt; bring to a boil, reduce heat to low and cook, covered, 35-40 minutes. (Water will be absorbed and rice will be tender when done.) Set aside to cool.
2. Toast walnuts in a 350°F oven for 15-20 minutes. (They will be fragrant and golden brown when done.) Set aside to cool.

continued ⟶

(Nutty Brown Rice, continued)

3. Prepare apple and stir together with lemon juice in a pretty serving bowl. (This will keep the apples from darkening.) Prepare and add the remaining veggies and the currants.
4. Combine dressing ingredients in a small bowl. Stir well to mix.
5. Combine cooled rice with apples and veggies in serving bowl. Add dressing and stir well. Stir in toasted walnuts. Ready to serve!

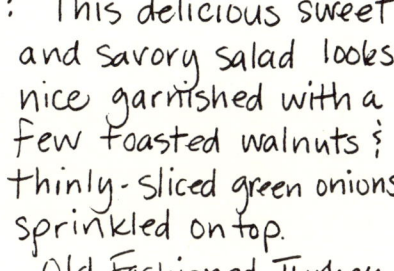

Serving Suggestion: This delicious sweet and savory salad looks nice garnished with a few toasted walnuts & thinly-sliced green onions sprinkled on top.
Old Fashioned Turkey Barley Soup and a warm Bran Muffin are good with Nutty Brown Rice.

- Curry powder is a blend of up to 20 different spices including coriander, fenugreek, cumin, cardamom, saffron, cloves, tamarind, red and black pepper, nutmeg, mace, chilies, and turmeric, which gives it the characteristic yellow color. Buy a very good brand of curry powder in small jars so it gets used fairly quickly. It will lose much of its flavor over time. Store in a glass jar in a cool, dark cupboard.

Mexi-Cali Rice
4-6 Servings

1 cup long-grain brown rice
½ tsp. salt
2 cups water

½ cup seeded and sliced green bell pepper
½ cup seeded and sliced red bell pepper
½ cup thinly-sliced red onion
1 small tomato, seeded and chopped
1 small zucchini, quartered lengthwise & sliced
1 small yellow squash, quartered lengthwise & sliced
¼ cup thinly-sliced green onion
¼ cup finely-chopped fresh parsley
¼ cup finely-chopped fresh cilantro
½-1 cup cooked pinto or kidney beans, optional

Dressing
¾ cup vegetable oil
¼ cup red wine vinegar
1 clove garlic, minced
1 jalapeño pepper, seeded and minced
½ tsp. salt
¼ tsp. black pepper
2 tsp. chili powder
1½ tsp. cumin
⅛ tsp. cayenne
3 drops Tabasco sauce

continued →

(Mexi-Cali Rice, continued)

1. In a medium saucepan, bring rice, salt, and water to a boil. Reduce heat to low and cook, covered, 35-40 minutes. (Water will be absorbed and rice will be tender when done.) Set aside to cool.
2. Prepare the veggies and place in a pretty serving bowl. Add the beans and stir together.
3. Prepare dressing ingredients. Combine in a blender or food processor; blend until smooth. (By hand: mince the garlic and jalapeño very fine. Put all ingredients in a large bowl; stir hard with a wire whisk until well mixed.)
4. Combine cooled rice with veggies and beans in serving bowl. Add the dressing and stir well.
5. Cover and let sit, refrigerated or at room temperature, until ready to serve.

Serving Suggestion: Serve this with Robert's Chili and cornbread - yes! They are delicious together. A frosty glass of ale... you're all set!

notes

Smoked Turkey Wild Rice
4-6 servings

1 cup long-grain brown rice
½ cup wild rice
½ tsp. salt
3 cups water

½ lb. smoked turkey breast, cubed
1 medium cucumber, peeled, seeded, and diced
½ cup thinly-sliced green onions
½ cup seeded and sliced green pepper
¼ cup finely-chopped fresh parsley
1 cup fresh or frozen peas
½ cup coarsely-chopped water chestnuts
1 (4-oz.) jar sliced, roasted pimentos, drained
  or ½ cup seeded and sliced red bell pepper

Dressing
1½ cups mayonnaise
2 Tbs. rice vinegar
2 tsp. Dijon mustard
½ tsp. marjoram
½ tsp. salt, more to taste
¼ tsp. black pepper

1. In a medium saucepan, bring rices, salt, and water to a boil. Reduce heat to low and cook, covered, 40-45 minutes. (Water will be absorbed and rice will be tender when done.) Set aside to cool.
2. Prepare the smoked turkey and veggies and place in a pretty serving bowl.

continued ⟶

(Smoked Turkey Wild Rice, continued)

3. Combine dressing ingredients in a small bowl. Stir well to mix.
4. Combine cooled rice with smoked turkey and veggies in serving bowl. Add the dressing and stir well.
5. Cover and refrigerate until ready to serve.

> **Serving Suggestion:** Serve on a fresh lettuce leaf garnished with a few green onion slices. Makes a meal when accompanied by steaming Minestrone soup and some fresh Buttermilk Oatmeal bread sticks.

> **Variations:** It's easy to make Smoked Salmon Wild Rice! Substitute equal amount smoked salmon for smoked turkey and 1/4 tsp. dill weed for the marjoram. (Fresh salmon, poached in a little white wine, is good, too!)

notes and new ideas ♥

Sesame Chicken Rice
4-6 servings

This salad contains Teriyaki Chicken which must be marinated 4-8 hours before cooking. (See "A few things about Teriyaki Chicken." p. 70)

Another of Tina Chow's salads and one of my favorites! A great salad to make when cucumbers are plentiful and taste best - fresh from a summer garden.

- 1 cup long-grain brown rice
- ½ cup wild rice
- ¼ tsp. salt
- 3 cups water

- ¼ cup sesame seeds
- 1 Tbs. sesame oil

- 1 lb. Teriyaki Chicken (p. 70), cut into bite-sized strips
- 3 large cucumbers, peeled, seeded, and chopped
- ¾ cup julienne red bell pepper
- ½ cup thinly-sliced green onion

Dressing
- ½ cup sesame oil
- ½ cup rice vinegar
- ¼ cup soy sauce
- ¼ cup Teriyaki Sauce (p. 33)

continued →

(Sesame Chicken Rice, continued)

1. In a medium saucepan, bring rices, salt and water to a boil. Reduce heat to low and cook, covered, for 35-40 minutes. (Water will be absorbed and rice will be tender when done.) Set aside to cool.
2. In a frying pan, toast sesame seeds in oil until golden brown. Set aside to cool.
3. Prepare Teriyaki Chicken and veggies and place in a pretty serving bowl. Set aside.
4. Combine dressing ingredients in a small bowl. Stir well to mix.
5. Combine cooled rice with chicken and veggies in serving bowl. Add dressing and stir well.
6. Cover and refrigerate until ready to serve.

- Wild rice, not truly a rice at all, is a long-grain marsh grass native to the Northern Great Lakes area. Deliciously nutty in flavor, it greatly enhances the taste, texture and appearance of salads. Although expensive to buy, a little goes a long way when mixed with brown rice.

- Chinese or Japanese rice vinegars are made from fermented rice and are milder, with a lower acid content, than Western vinegars. They range in flavor from very mild (almost clear in color) to very sweet (dark purple). For these salads use a mild rice vinegar, clear to light amber in color.

San Francisco Rice
2-4 servings

1 cup long-grain white rice
½ tsp. salt
2 cup water

½ cup seeded and chopped green bell pepper
½ cup sliced celery
¼ cup thinly-sliced green onion
¼ cup finely-chopped fresh parsley
¼ cup pimento-stuffed green olives, sliced
1 (6-oz) jar marinated artichoke hearts, drained (reserve marinade) and sliced
1 (4-oz) jar sliced, roasted pimentos, drained
   or ½ cup seeded and chopped red bell pepper

Dressing
   1-1½ cups mayonnaise
   reserved marinade from artichoke hearts
   1-2 tsp. curry powder
   ½ tsp. salt
   ¼ tsp. white pepper

1. In a medium saucepan bring rice, salt, and water to a boil. Reduce heat to low and cook covered 15-20 minutes. (Water will be absorbed and rice tender when done.) Set aside to cool.
2. Prepare veggies and place in a pretty serving bowl.
3. Combine dressing ingredients in a small bowl. Stir well.
4. Combine cooled rice with veggies in serving bowl. Add dressing and stir well.
5. Cover and let sit, refrigerated or at room temperature, until ready to serve.

Leslie's Zingy Potato Salad
5-6 side servings

Contributed by another very creative crew member Leslie Gardner, Leslie's Zingy Potato Salad is a favorite at the Café (among crew and customers alike). Delicious served chilled or at room temperature.

2 lbs. red potatoes, "au naturel" (unpeeled and uncut)

Dressing
- 1 cup mayonnaise
- ¼ cup Vinaigrette dressing (p.25)
- 2 Tbs. Dijon mustard
- 1 large dill pickle, coarsely chopped
- ½ cup thinly-sliced green onions
- ½ tsp. <u>each</u> salt and black pepper

1. In a medium sauce pan cover whole potatoes with cold water. Bring to a boil, reduce heat to a healthy simmer, and cook until tender, 15-20 minutes. Drain. Set aside to cool.
2. In a medium bowl combine dressing ingredients. Stir.
3. When potatoes are cool enough to handle, cut into large bite-sized pieces and place in a pretty serving bowl. Add dressing and stir well.
4. Cover and let sit, refrigerated or at room temperature, until ready to serve. Adjust seasonings, adding more salt & pepper, if desired.

"If you want
a golden rule
that will fit everyone,
this is it:
Have nothing
in your houses
that you do not
know to be useful,
or believe
to be beautiful."

William Morris 1880
"The Beauty of Life"

Quiches

- An Introduction 109
- Quiche Pastry 114
- Quiche Custard 116
- Cheese and Onion Pie 117
- Savory Mushroom Quiche 118
- Broccoli-Cheddar Quiche 119
- Broccoli, Fresh Herbs, and Cheeses Quiche 120
- Spanish Quiche 122
- Autumn Vegetable Quiche 124
- Quiche Lorraine 125
- Spinach Ricotta Pie 126
- Savory Squash Pie 128
- Sicilian Quiche 130
- Create-A-Quiche 131

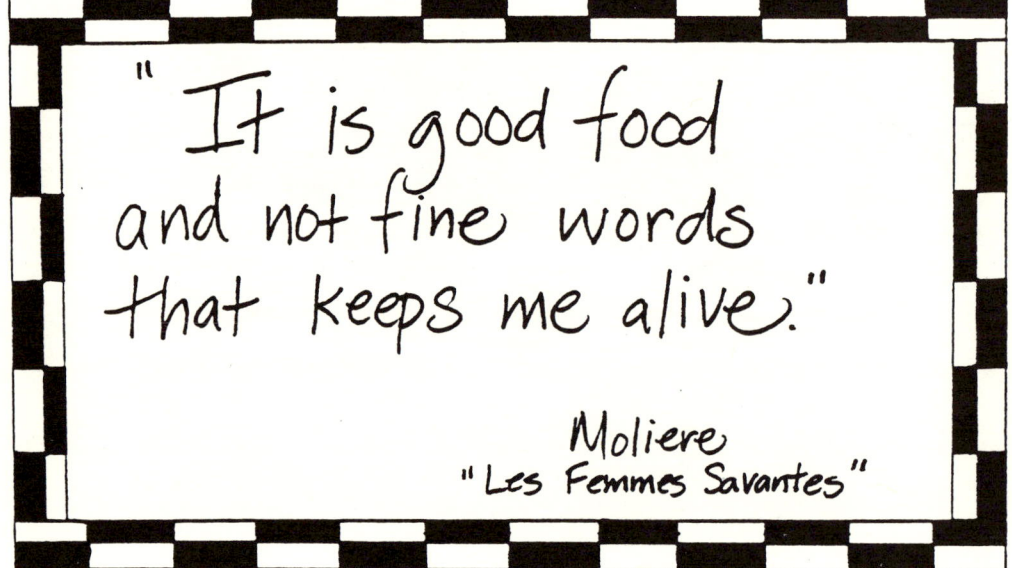

"It is good food
and not fine words
that keeps me alive."

Moliere
"Les Femmes Savantes"

Quiches

Long will I remember my first quiche-making experience of many years ago. I was really intimidated by the prospect of making a crust. I knew mine would never be as flaky as the ones I admired. Strangely enough, when I finally mustered up the courage to make a winter vegetable quiche with carrots, onion, broccoli, and mushrooms, the crust turned out OK (edible, anyway). The filling, on the other hand, was a total failure! I hadn't sautéed the veggies so they released their moisture during baking. When I took my quiche from the oven it was a soggy mess. The crust was overly-brown on the edges but soggy on the bottom. Because of the excess vegetable water, the custard never did set up. To top things off, I cut it too soon and literally had to spoon it out. My husband, bless his loving heart, ate it, saying the next one would be better. He was right!

    I laugh looking back on it now. The mistakes I made were easily overcome and quiche-making seems so simple to me now. The reason: I know the rules. There are several to obey if you want to make a perfect quiche, but they're not difficult. If you're a new cook, read this and follow my instructions; it may save you from having to learn the hard way. If you have made your share of quiches, this may teach you a few new tricks or just give you some new ideas to play with.

    Carefully read the recipe and instructions for Quiche Pastry (p.114) and Quiche Custard (p.116) That and the

continued →

following information will help you make a perfect quiche.

The Pastry: Make your crust pastry first and let it rest in the refrigerator for 20-30 minutes before rolling it out. Or get a jump on the game and make enough for 3 or 4 crusts at a time, divide into equal pieces, form into balls, flatten slightly, and wrap individually in plastic wrap. Store in the freezer until you need them. Simply defrost in your refrigerator overnight, on your counter in a few hours, or in your microwave in a few minutes.

Rolling and Forming: Choose the largest flat surface in your kitchen to roll the pastry on. Sprinkle the surface generously with flour and place pastry ball in the center. Sprinkle more flour on top and, using a rolling pin, roll out a large circle 16" wide and 1/8"-1/4" thick. Apply even pressure and roll from the center out in all directions to form a nice round circle. Brush off the excess flour. (Purchase a nice, wide pastry brush to do this; it works so well!) Fold the rolled-out pastry in half and gently place in the buttered quiche pan. Unfold it to completely cover the pan. It will hang loosely over the sides. Gently press the pastry into the bottom and sides of the pan. Fold the overhang under itself to form a rim, and gently squeeze it together with your fingers and thumb to "flute" it. I make what I call the "sunflower design": Place

continued →

thumb and forefinger on the outside edge of the rim of pastry. Place your other thumb on the inside edge and press down and out, between your other thumb and forefinger, with a gentle but firm pressure. This will create a pretty sunflower petal design. Go around the entire rim of dough doing this until you have a complete circle of petals.

Once the crust is formed refrigerate it while you make the custard and filling. A cold crust holds its shape better as it bakes and turns out tender and flaky.

If you are (or want to be) a "wise cook," the always-prepared-never-know-when-you-might-want-to-pop-a-quiche-in-the-oven-type, make up several rolled out and fluted quiche crusts at a time and freeze them, pans and all, individually wrapped in plastic bags. Pull one out when you need it! They can go straight from the freezer into the oven, stopping first to receive the quiche filling, of course. You'll be so pleased with yourself. Don't despair if you're not there yet. It takes years to reach this pinnacle of "cuisine-dom." You can get there if you want to! ★

*note: These crusts can also be used for sweet pies!

The Filling: If you are using watery vegetables in your filling, you must pre-cook them first. Sauté until tender, then add to your filling. Vegetables that need to be sautéed are onion, broccoli <u>stalk</u>, zucchini, peppers, carrot, mushroom, asparagus, celery, cauliflower,

continued ⟶

and tomatoes. These vegetables can be used uncooked: green onions, parsley, broccoli florets, canned pimentos, black olives, and marinated artichoke hearts.

The Custard: Use a wire whisk or a slotted spoon to mix the custard. I combine my seasonings and flour (which is added as a binder) with a small amount of milk from the recipe, mixing until smooth, before adding to the eggs and milk. This helps incorporate them more smoothly into the custard. Whisk the custard well until it starts to form a froth on the surface. If you don't pour it immediately, restir before doing so.

The Baking: Always preheat the oven and make sure that it's up to temperature and evenly hot. I bake my quiches at 375°F. It gives them a crisper and flakier crust. Always bake on the lowest shelf in the oven, as close to the oven floor as possible, to prevent a soggy bottom crust. Quiche takes 35-45 minutes to bake. When done, the crust will be a rich golden brown and the filling lightly browned and set. Try to develop a "sense" for when it's done by its appearance, fragrance, and the way it responds when you gently press on the center.

Cooling: The quiche must cool 8-10 minutes before you cut it.

continued ⟶

Cutting: At the Café we cut our quiches into 6 generous servings. You can cut yours into as many (or few) pieces as you want. Use a sharp serated knife and a sawing motion to cut quiche. This keeps the top from tearing and creates a better presentation.

Storing: Quiche will keep up to 4 days in the refrigerator and makes delicious leftovers. It's so easy to pop a piece of quiche in the microwave, toaster oven, or oven and have a hot, nourishing meal. Quiche is great for breakfast, too! I have had passable results with freezing quiche. It tends to become soggy as it defrosts so I wouldn't serve it for a special dinner. But, for a quick meal that is wholesome and hot, it's quite acceptable.

Notes and inspirations ★

Quiche Pastry
one 10-inch crust

This is where many fall apart when it comes to making quiche. Believe me - it's not that difficult. (Read the introduction on p. 109 for a smile.) All it takes to make a perfect quiche is a good general knowledge of the procedure, and <u>practice</u>. I'll supply the knowledge; the practice is up to you. I've never heard of anyone tiring of quiche (except my husband, but that was only after I'd brought it home several lazy nights in a row). Decide to make it once a week - your family and friends will love you for it! I'll provide enough recipes to keep you going for a couple of months.

> 1½ cups unbleached flour
> ¼ tsp. salt
> 6 Tbs. cold butter, cut into small pieces
> 3 Tbs. vegetable shortening, cut into small pieces
> 1 egg, lightly beaten
> 3 Tbs. ice water

1. In a large bowl mix flour and salt together. Using a pastry knife or 2 forks, cut butter and shortening into the flour until it resembles coarse cornmeal. (There will still be some tiny lumps of butter.)
    Food processor instructions: Put flour and salt in bowl with metal blade and pulse. Add pieces of butter and shortening and pulse 5-6 times.

continued ⟶

(Quiche Pastry, continued)

2. In a small bowl, whisk eggs and ice water together. Add to the flour/butter mixture with a fork until it just starts to hold together.
    Food processor instructions: Add egg/ice water mixture through the feed tube into the flour/butter mixture and pulse 5-6 times.

3. Turn the pastry out onto a lightly floured counter and pat into a flat circle about 1 inch thick. Refrigerate at least 20 minutes before rolling out. (Pastry can be refrigerated overnight or frozen for later use. See pgs. 110, 111.)

4. Sprinkle more flour onto your work space and, with a rolling pin, roll the pastry out into a circle 1/8-1/4" thick. It should be about 16" in diameter. (It's okay to be generous with the flour - it makes rolling easier. Just remember to brush it all off before you line the pan.)

5. Butter a 10" pie tin. Place the crust in the pan and press gently to line the inside. Pastry should hang evenly over the rim and drape down to the counter. Tuck the overhang underneath to form a thick edge. Make a decorative pattern in this edge with your fingers or a fork. Refrigerate your crust while you make the filling.

. . . .

Notes ♥

Quiche Custard
one 10-inch quiche

This is my all-time favorite quiche custard, so we use it daily at the Café. We make many different quiches and have an assortment for sale at all times. All, except for 2 savory pies, use this custard in the filling. It's delicious, not overly rich (we use 2% milk), and really puffs up nicely in the oven.

> 4 eggs
> 2 Tbs. flour
> 1/2 tsp. salt
> 1/2 tsp. white pepper
> 1/4 tsp. nutmeg
> 1 3/4 cup milk (2%, whole, or Half & Half - your choice)

1. In a large bowl, beat eggs until frothy with a wire whisk or a mixing spoon.
2. In a small bowl, mix together flour, salt, pepper, and nutmeg with 2 Tbs. of the milk. When smooth, beat into the eggs.
3. Add remaining milk to egg mixture, beating well with the whisk or spoon. (Custard will be frothy on top when done.)
4. Stir until blended again right before pouring into quiche crust.

Cheese and Onion Pie
one 10" quiche ★ 6-8 servings

1 quiche crust, unbaked (p. 114)
1 cup shredded Swiss cheese
½ cup shredded Cheddar cheese

1 Tbs. butter or vegetable oil
1 medium onion, halved and thinly-sliced
¼ cup thinly-sliced green onions
¼ cup minced fresh parsley
¼ tsp. salt
⅛ tsp. white pepper

1 cup shredded Cheddar cheese
1 recipe quiche custard (p. 116)
1 Tbs. thinly-sliced green onions
1 Tbs. grated Parmesan cheese

1. Evenly distribute first 1½ cups shredded cheeses onto the bottom of prepared crust. Place in the refrigerator until ready to use. Preheat oven to 375°F.
2. In a large wide pot or frying pan, sauté veggies and seasonings in butter or oil, over medium heat, for 7-10 minutes. (Onion will be tender and lightly browned when done.)
3. Take crust from refrigerator. Spoon onion mixture evenly over cheese in crust. Place remaining cheese on top of onions and gently pour custard on. Sprinkle remaining green onions and Parmesan cheese on top (for decoration).
4. Bake on lowest shelf in oven for 40-45 minutes. (Crust will be a lovely golden brown and filling will be browned and firm to the touch when done.)
5. Cool 8-10 minutes before cutting and serving.

Savory Mushroom Quiche
one 10" quiche ♥ 6-8 servings

1 quiche crust, unbaked (p. 114)
1 cup shredded Swiss cheese

1 Tbs. butter or vegetable oil
½ cup thinly-sliced onion
1½ cup sliced fresh mushrooms
¼ tsp. salt
¼ tsp. black pepper
½ tsp. thyme
1 Tbs. dry sherry

1 cup shredded Swiss cheese
1 recipe quiche custard (p. 116)

1. Evenly distribute first cup Swiss cheese onto the bottom of prepared crust. Place in the refrigerator until ready to use. Preheat oven to 375°F.
2. In a large wide pot or frying pan, sauté onion in butter or oil, over medium heat, for 5 minutes. Add mushrooms and seasonings and sauté for 5 minutes more. (When done, onions will be transparent and golden brown, mushrooms tender and shrunken, and liquid from mushrooms will be evaporated.) Stir in sherry and remove from heat.
3. Take crust from refrigerator. Spoon mushroom mixture evenly over cheese in crust. Place remaining cheese on top and gently pour custard on.
4. Bake on lowest shelf of oven for 40-45 minutes (crust will be a lovely golden brown and filling will be browned and firm to the touch when done.)
5. Cool 8-10 minutes before cutting and serving.

Broccoli-Cheddar Quiche
one 10" quiche ☙ 8-10 servings

1 quiche crust, unbaked (p. 114)
1 cup shredded Swiss cheese
½ cup shredded Cheddar cheese

1½ cups. broccoli florets

1 cup shredded Cheddar cheese
1 recipe quiche custard (p. 116)

1. Evenly distribute first 1½ cups shredded cheeses onto the bottom of prepared crust. Place in the refrigerator until ready to use. Preheat oven to 375°F.
2. In a double boiler or small pan, steam or blanch broccoli for 2 minutes. Drain and pat dry.
   ♥note: Broccoli florets can be used raw. They will cook during the baking time. Steaming or blanching brings out the color and makes them slightly more succulent!
3. Take crust from refrigerator. Evenly spread broccoli over cheese in crust. Place remaining cheeses on top of broccoli and gently pour custard on.
4. Bake on lowest shelf in oven for 40-45 minutes (Crust will be a lovely golden brown and filling will be browned and firm to the touch when done.)
5. Cool 8-10 minutes before cutting and serving.

Broccoli, Fresh Herbs, & Cheeses Quiche
one 10" quiche ☀ 6-8 servings

A sensational quiche! A warning: It's very rich, so you will want to serve small slices with a fresh green salad and a cold white wine or iced tea.

1 quiche crust, unbaked (p. 114)

1 cup broccoli florets

6 oz. cream cheese, at room temperature
2 Tbs. unbleached flour
3 eggs
1½ cups shredded Swiss cheese
2 Tbs. sliced green onions
2 Tbs. minced fresh parsley
1 Tbs. minced fresh basil (or 1 tsp. dried)
1 tsp. minced fresh marjoram (or ¼ tsp. dried)
1 tsp. minced fresh tarragon (or ¼ tsp. dried)
1 Tbs. grated Parmesan cheese
¼ tsp. <u>each</u> salt, white pepper, & nutmeg

1½ cups milk

1 Tbs. grated Parmesan cheese
a pinch <u>each</u> minced basil, marjoram & tarragon

continued →

(Broccoli, Fresh Herbs, and Cheeses Quiche, continued)

1. Place prepared quiche crust in refrigerator until needed. Preheat oven to 375°F.
2. Steam or blanch broccoli florets for 2 minutes. Cool, drain, and pat dry.
   - ♥note: Broccoli florets do not have to be steamed or blanched before using for quiche. They will cook during the baking period. Precooking brings out their color and makes them more succulent.
3. In a large bowl, by hand or with an electric mixer, beat cream cheese until smooth. Add flour, then eggs, one at a time. Beat until smooth, scraping sides of bowl often. Add other ingredients (except for broccoli, milk, last Tbs. of Parmesan and pinches of herbs) and blend well. Add milk, ½ cup at a time, blending well between additions. Stir vigorously for 1 minute. Stir in broccoli florets.
4. Remove crust from refrigerator and spread broccoli-cream cheese mixture evenly over crust. Sprinkle remaining Parmesan cheese and pinches of herbs on top.
5. Bake on lowest shelf in oven for 40-45 minutes. (Crust will be a nice golden brown and filling will be browned and firm to the touch when done.)
6. Cool 8-10 minutes before cutting and serving.

> Serving Suggestion: Makes a fabulous appetizer or buffet selection. Bake in small unsweetened tart shells (purchased in the freezer section of the grocery) or cut quiche into thin slices. Can be served hot or cold.

Spanish Quiche
one 10" quiche ~ 6-8 servings

1 quiche crust, unbaked (p. 114)
½ cup shredded Cheddar cheese
½ cup shredded Jack cheese

1 Tbs. butter or vegetable oil
½ cup sliced onion
½ cup seeded and sliced green bell pepper
¼ tsp. salt
¼ tsp. _each_ chili powder and cumin
½ tsp. oregano
⅛ tsp. black pepper

1 (2 oz.) jar sliced pimentos, drained
¼ cup sliced black olives
1 Tbs. sliced green onions
1 Tbs. minced parsley
1 Tbs. minced cilantro, optional

½ cup shredded Cheddar cheese
½ cup shredded Jack cheese
1 recipe quiche custard (p. 116)
a dusting of paprika

1. Evenly distribute first cup shredded cheeses onto the bottom of prepared crust. Place in refrigerator until ready to use. Preheat oven to 375°F.
2. In a large wide pot or frying pan, sauté onion and green pepper in butter or oil over medium heat for 3 minutes. Add seasonings and sauté 3-5 minutes more, until tender. Remove from the heat and stir in pimento, black olives,

continued ⟶

(Spanish Quiche, continued)

green onions, parsley and optional cilantro.
3. Take crust from refrigerator. Spoon veggie mixture evenly over the cheese in crust. Place remaining cheeses on top of veggies and gently pour custard on. Top with a dusting of paprika (for decoration).
4. Bake on lowest shelf in oven for 40-45 minutes. (Crust will be a lovely golden brown and filling browned and firm to the touch when done.)
5. Cool 8-10 minutes before cutting and serving.

....

Notes ←

Autumn Vegetable Quiche
one 10" quiche ❀ 6-8 servings

1 quiche crust, unbaked (p. 114)
1 cup shredded Swiss cheese

1 Tbs. butter or vegetable oil
½ cup sliced onion
½ cup chopped broccoli
¼ cup seeded and sliced green bell pepper
¼ cup seeded and sliced red bell pepper
¼ tsp. each   salt, black pepper, basil, and marjoram

1 cup shredded Swiss cheese
1 recipe quiche custard (p. 116)

1. Evenly distribute first cup Swiss cheese onto the bottom of prepared crust. Place in the refrigerator until ready to use. Preheat oven to 375°F.
2. In a large wide pot or frying pan sauté veggies and seasonings in butter or oil, over medium heat, for 7-10 minutes, until tender.
3. Take crust from refrigerator. Spoon veggie mixture evenly over cheese in crust. Place remaining cheese on top of veggies and gently pour custard on.
4. Bake on lowest shelf in oven for 40-45 minutes. (Crust will be a lovely golden brown and filling will be browned and firm to the touch when done.)
5. Cool 8-10 minutes before cutting and serving.

Quiche Lorraine
one 10" quiche ☼ 6-8 servings

1 quiche crust, unbaked (p. 114)
1 cup shredded Swiss cheese
1-2 cups thinly-sliced cooked lean ham, cut into strips

1 cup shredded Swiss cheese
1 recipe quiche custard (p. 116)
1 Tbs. grated Parmesan cheese
1 tsp. sliced green onions, optional

1. Preheat oven to 375°F. Evenly distribute first cup Swiss cheese onto the bottom of prepared crust. Evenly spread ham over the cheese. Place remaining cheese on top of the ham and gently pour custard on. Sprinkle Parmesan cheese and optional green onions on top (for decoration).
2. Bake on lowest shelf in oven for 40-45 minutes. (Crust will be golden brown and filling will be browned and firm to the touch when done.)
3. Cool 8-10 minutes before cutting and serving.

....

Notes ☼

Spinach Ricotta Pie
one 10" quiche ✷ 6-8 servings

Adapted from Mollie Katzen's Moosewood Cookbook. I've added a few things and spiced it up a bit. It's <u>delicious</u> but how can you miss when you start out with such an excellent idea! Serve with a little fresh applesauce or homemade chutney.

1 quiche crust, unbaked (p.114)

1 Tbs. butter or vegetable oil
1 small onion, chopped
1 small green bell pepper, chopped
1 tsp. salt
1 tsp. basil
½ tsp. black pepper
⅛ - ¼ tsp. cayenne
¾ lb. fresh spinach, stemmed, washed, and chopped

1 lb. ricotta cheese
3 eggs
3 Tbs. flour
¼ tsp. nutmeg
½ cup shredded Swiss cheese

2 Tbs. grated Parmesan cheese

1. Place prepared quiche crust in the refrigerator while you prepare filling. Preheat oven to 375°F.
2. In a large, wide pot or frying pan sauté onion and green pepper in butter or oil, over medium heat, for 7 minutes. Add seasonings and spinach and cook

continued →

(Spinach Ricotta Pie, continued)

5 minutes more. (Spinach will be wilted and excess moisture evaporated.)

3. In a large bowl combine remaining ingredients (except grated Parmesan). Mix well. Stir in spinach mixture (scrape pan with a spatula to retrieve all the seasonings).
4. Take crust from refrigerator. Spread the filling evenly over the crust. Top with grated Parmesan.
5. Bake on lowest shelf of oven for 50-55 minutes. (Crust and Parmesan will be a lovely golden brown and filling firm to the touch when done.)
6. Cool 8-10 minutes before serving.

· ·

Notes ☆

Savory Squash Pie
one 10" quiche 6-8 servings

1 quiche crust, unbaked (p. 114)

1 Tbs. butter or vegetable oil
1 medium onion, halved and sliced
1 tsp. salt
½ tsp. basil
½ tsp. black pepper
⅛ - ¼ tsp. cayenne

2 cups squash puree (Use pumpkin, acorn, butternut, delicata or any firm-fleshed winter squash. Boil or steam until tender, drain well and mash.)
or 1 (16-oz) can solid pack pumpkin
3 eggs
¼ cup Half & Half or milk
⅛ tsp. nutmeg
1 cup shredded Swiss cheese

2 Tbs. grated Parmesan cheese

1. Place prepared quiche crust in the refrigerator while you prepare filling. Preheat oven to 375°F.
2. In a large, wide pot or frying pan sauté onion in butter or oil, over medium heat, for 7-10 minutes. (Onion will be tender and lightly browned when done.) Add seasonings, green onions, and parsley. Sauté 1 minute more.
3. In a large bowl combine remaining ingredients (except grated Parmesan). Stir in the sautéed veggies (scrape pan with spatula to retrieve all the seasonings). Mix well.

continued →

(Savory Squash Pie, continued)

4. Take crust from refrigerator. Spread the filling evenly over the crust. Top with grated Parmesan.
5. Bake on lowest shelf of oven for 50-55 minutes. (Crust and Parmesan will be a lovely golden brown and filling firm to the touch when done.)
6. Cool 8-10 minutes before cutting and serving.

· ·

Notes

Sicilian Quiche
one 10" quiche • 6-8 servings

1 quiche crust, unbaked (p. 114)
1 cup shredded Swiss cheese

½ cup chopped cooked lean ham
½ cup marinated artichoke hearts, drained
¼ cup sliced black olives
1 (2 oz.) jar sliced roasted pimentos
2 Tbs. sliced green onions
1 Tbs. chopped fresh parsley

1 cup shredded Swiss cheese
1 recipe quiche custard (p. 116)
1 Tbs. grated Parmesan cheese

1. Preheat oven to 375°F. Evenly distribute first cup Swiss cheese onto bottom of prepared crust. Evenly spread ham over cheese and proceed with the veggies, distributing evenly in the quiche. Place remaining cheese on top of the ham and veggies and gently pour custard on. Sprinkle Parmesan cheese on top.
2. Bake on lowest shelf in oven for 40-45 minutes. (Crust will be golden brown and filling will be browned and firm to the touch when done.)
3. Cool 8-10 minutes before cutting and serving.

Create-A-Quiche

Here are a few other food combinations to try in a quiche. Start with our crust (p. 114) and end with our custard (p. 116) but nestled in between try these:

HAM & BROCCOLI: thinly-sliced ham, shredded Swiss cheese, broccoli florets. Top with grated Parmesan and thinly-sliced green onions.

- - - - - - - - - - - - - - - - - - -

TURKEY & CHEDDAR: thinly-sliced breast of turkey, shredded Swiss cheese, shredded Cheddar cheese

♥ ♥ ♥ ♥ ♥ ♥ ♥ ♥ ♥ ♥ ♥ ♥ ♥ ♥ ♥

TERIYAKI CHICKEN: sautéed onion and green bell pepper, sliced teriyaki chicken (p. 70) shredded jack cheese. Top with sliced green onions.

▲ ▲ ▲ ▲ ▲ ▲ ▲ ▲ ▲ ▲ ▲ ▲ ▲ ▲ ▲

BRIE: a thin wedge of Brie cheese per piece, shredded Swiss cheese, thinly-sliced roasted pimento. Minced fresh parsley on top.

★ ★ ★ ★ ★ ★ ★ ★ ★ ★ ★ ★ ★ ★ ★

GREEK: sliced artichoke hearts, a little chopped feta cheese, grated Parmesan cheese, black olives, diced pimento. Top with tomato slices.

• • • • • • • • • • • • • • • • •

FRESH ASPARAGUS (& HAM) ⟶ blanched fresh asparagus, shredded Swiss cheese (add thinly-sliced ham)

Feel free to use your own favorite food combinations. After all, who are you trying to please? Ask friends and family for suggestions, too. I find, given the chance, everyone has something to say about food!

"Without bread
even a palace is sad,
but with it
a pine tree is paradise."

Slavic proverb

Breads & Muffins

- An Introduction 134
- Cranberry-Orange Muffins 140
- Lemon-Pecan Muffins 142
- Bran Muffins 144
- Poppyseed Muffins 146
- Cappuccino Chip Muffins 148
- Savory Garden Muffins 150
- Mexican Corn Muffins 152
- Gingerbread 154
- Buttermilk Oatmeal Bread 156
- Café Cornbread 159
- Irish Soda Bread 160

Breads & Muffins

While in high school, I dated a boy who had a Polish grandmother we all called Busha. Busha was a wise, little old woman who lived in a small house with a large garden that produced beautiful flowers and large succulent vegetables. And she loved to bake bread. We spent hours with Busha, listening to her stories and advice, helping with her garden, and eating her long-simmered soups and fresh-from-the-oven breads. A homemaker all her life (she was in her 80's when I knew her), Busha was very practical about her job. Her family needed to be cared for and she did this with hard work, warm hospitality, and her old-fashioned, hearty cooking. This practicality extended to her bread making, but she also had an air of the artist about her when she baked. She worked with much enthusiasm and her steaming, fragrant loaves were certainly a work of art to be enjoyed by the mind, body, and soul.

Busha inspired me with her well-kept kitchen, her loaves of fresh bread, and her happy, lively attitude toward the whole process. Baking is also my favorite field of cooking and I intend to devote my next book to it. However, this book, mainly about salads and soups would not be complete without a few breads to balance and complement the dishes. I have chosen the following breads and muffins for their versatility, tastiness, and especially their ease of preparation. They are mainly "quick breads" and can be made and popped in the oven in no time at all.

Baking Basics

A few helpful hints to make the process smoother and the product more delectable!

1. It's important to have all your ingredients at room temperature. This ensures that they will combine well. My mother-in-law, Ginny Williams, has a good hint for warming eggs: she pops them in her bra for a few minutes! (Kitchen ingenuity at its best!)
2. Read your recipe all the way through before starting.
3. Have all your ingredients and measuring implements assembled before you begin.
4. Grease and flour your pans. Plain shortening dusted with flour works best to prevent batter from sticking.
5. Preheat the oven to the temperature specified in the recipe 10-15 minutes before you're ready to bake.
6. Use a knife to level ingredients in measuring cups.
7. Use the lid of the container or a small knife to level ingredients in measuring spoons. Use the palm of your hand to smooth any lumpy ingredients, such as baking soda.
8. Crack eggs into a bowl before adding to check for freshness and any errant shells.
9. To avoid a cornbread or cake "peaking" in the center during baking, use a spatula to make a slight indentation, pushing the batter from the center gently to the sides. When it bakes it should become level.

continued →

10. The suggested baking times in the recipes are only an approximation since oven temperatures vary. Use a cake tester or a long wooden toothpick to check for doneness. Test by poking it in the thickest part (usually the center). It's done when the tester comes out clean.

11. Serve your bread warm from the oven if possible, but cool for 10-15 minutes before slicing. To store, wrap with plastic and refrigerate. Breads will keep for a few days. To store for a longer time, double wrap with plastic, place in a heavy plastic bag, and freeze. Whether you refrigerate or freeze bread, it's nice to reheat it in a preheated oven for 5-10 minutes before serving.

Leavening Agents

Agents that are used to lighten the texture and increase the volume of baked goods. When combined with a liquid they form carbon dioxide bubbles in the batter or dough causing it to rise before and/or during baking.

Baking Soda (sodium bicarbonate): Baking soda has no leavening power when used alone. It needs an acid ingredient like buttermilk, lemon juice, or molasses to produce the carbon dioxide bubbles that will raise your baked good and give it a "tender crumb." It is "fast-acting" and "moisture-activated," so mix the

continued →

baking soda with your dry ingredients first. Have your oven preheated so the dough or batter can be put into the oven immediately after preparing. Rule-of-thumb proportions: use 1 tsp. baking soda for each cup of buttermilk in the recipe.

Before using baking soda, break up any lumps that have formed.

Baking soda contains over 800 mg. of sodium per teaspoon.

Cream of tartar (potassium bitartrate): This is most commonly used as an acid ingredient in baking powder and also as a flavor and consistency enhancer in candies and a stabilizer in cooking. The white crystals that form as wine grapes ferment are cream of tartar.

Baking powder: Tartrate and "Double-Acting" are the two most commonly used baking powders. Both contain cornstarch as a filler.

Tartrate baking powder is made from sodium bicarbonate (baking soda) and potassium bitartrate (cream of tartar). It's "fast-acting," working immediately on contact with liquid and at room temperature. When using, make sure you have the oven preheated, to bake immediately.

"Double-acting" baking powder is made from sodium bicarbonate (baking soda) plus sodium aluminum sulfate and calcium acid phosphate. It also begins to work when mixed with a

continued →

liquid but the major rising occurs when the batter becomes hot in the oven. This is the most common baking powder used today due to the increased stability of the "heat-activated" rising.

To make your own baking powder mix ½ tsp. cream of tartar and ⅓ tsp. baking soda to equal the rising power of 1 tsp. baking powder. Remember that this produces the "fast-acting" baking powder and must be baked right away.

Baking powder doesn't last forever and should be tested from time to time. Mix 1 tsp. baking powder in ⅓ cup hot water. Use only if it bubbles healthily.

Baking powder contains 330 mg. of sodium per teaspoon. For comparison, table salt (sodium chloride) has close to 2,000 mg. of sodium per teaspoon.

Bakers Yeast: A living, microscopic, single cell organism (3200 billion to the pound!) which produces carbon dioxide when mixed with a warm liquid and a "food" (usually sugar). These carbon dioxide bubbles grow and multiply in bread dough or batter making it rise before and during baking.

Of the several forms of yeast available today, we'll concentrate on the two most commonly used as leaveners in baking: active dry yeast and compressed fresh yeast.

Active dry yeast is dehydrated yeast that is dormant until mixed with warm liquid

continued →

(100°-110°F). When mixed with the batter or dough the cells multiply and grow, leavening the baked good. You can purchase 1/4 oz. envelopes (or "packages" as referred to in recipes) or 4 oz. jars. Store in a cool, dark place or, better yet, in the freezer.

Compressed fresh yeast is live yeast that is perishable and must be refrigerated until ready to use. It is moist, greyish-tan in color and comes in tiny 1/2 oz. square cakes or larger 1 lb. blocks. It can be stored in the refrigerator for 1-2 weeks and frozen for up to 2 months. If frozen, defrost at room temperature and use immediately. We use fresh yeast in our baking at the Café. I prefer the flavor of fresh yeast in baked goods - a subtle difference most definitely. At home I use active dry yeast that I buy in 4 oz. jars and store in the freezer. The ease of storing and using dry yeast makes it a better choice for the home baker.

Proof your yeast before you use it. This is a test to show that the yeast is, in fact, alive and happy. Dissolve the yeast in warm water (100°-110°F) with a little sugar in it. Set aside for 5-10 minutes. It will expand and become foamy if it's alive and capable of leavening. Never dissolve yeast in water that has had salt added to it. Salt inhibits the growth of yeast and should always be added with the flour.

Cranberry-Orange Muffins

10 large or 12 medium muffins

My very talented sister, Maureen O'Shea (she's also a MD and makes beautiful needlework to sell at the Café during the holidays) created this fruity and tart muffin.

★ Preheat oven to 350°F. ★ Generously grease muffin tin ★

- 1 cup finely-chopped cranberries
- 1 cup granulated sugar

- 2 cups unbleached all-purpose flour
- 2 tsp. baking powder
- ½ tsp. baking soda
- ½ tsp. salt

- ⅓ cup vegetable oil
- ⅔ cup orange juice
- 1 large egg, lightly beaten
- 1 tsp. vanilla extract
- ½ tsp. grated orange rind

- ½ cup chopped walnuts

1. In a small bowl combine cranberries and sugar. Mix thoroughly. Let sit 15 minutes.
2. In a large mixing bowl combine dry ingredients. Mix thoroughly.
3. In a smaller bowl combine oil, juice, egg, vanilla, and orange rind. Beat until mixture becomes slightly frothy. Stir in cranberry-sugar mixture.

continued →

(Cranberry-Orange Muffins, continued)

4. Combine wet ingredients and dry ingredients in large mixing bowl. Add the walnuts and gently stir just until dry ingredients are moistened. A few lumps may remain — that's OK!
5. Spoon batter into greased muffin tin. Lightly sprinkle granulated sugar on top. Fill 3/4 full to make 12 or to the top to make 10. Bake in preheated oven for 18-22 minutes or until a toothpick inserted into middle of muffin comes out clean.

🍎 Orange (or lemon) rind adds a heightened flavor and aroma to baked goods. After washing the fruit thoroughly, remove the outermost layer of skin, also called the zest, with a citrus zester, vegetable peeler or a sharp paring knife. Use only the colored portion of the skin; the white membrane underneath, called the pith, is bitter.

· ·

Notes 🍒

Lemon-Pecan Muffins
12 large muffins

Here's another of my sister Maureen's lovely muffins. Very lemony, tart, and fragrant, it's delicious with soup or salad as well as coffee or tea.

★ Preheat oven to 350°F. ★ Generously grease muffin tin ★

3 cups unbleached all-purpose flour
2 cups granulated sugar
1½ tsp. baking powder
¼ tsp. salt
⅔ cup finely-chopped pecans

2 large eggs, lightly beaten
⅔ cup Half & Half
juice from 2 large lemons plus
  enough water to make ⅔ cup liquid
⅔ cup melted butter
1 tsp. grated lemon rind

1. In a large mixing bowl combine dry ingredients including pecans. Mix thoroughly.
2. In a smaller bowl combine wet ingredients, including lemon rind. Beat until mixture becomes slightly frothy.
3. Combine wet ingredients and dry ingredients in large mixing bowl. Gently stir just until dry ingredients are moistened. A few lumps may remain - that's OK!

continued ⟶

(Lemon-Pecan Muffins, continued)

4. Spoon batter into greased muffin tin. Lightly sprinkle granulated sugar on top. Bake in preheated oven for 25-30 minutes or until a toothpick inserted into middle of a muffin comes out clean.

· ·

Notes ♥

Bran Muffins
12 large muffins

This is one of the first recipes I developed when getting ready to open the Café. It holds a special place in my heart...tastes good, too!

★ Preheat oven to 350°F. ★ Generously grease muffin tin ★

½ cup raisins
1 cup hot water

½ cup butter or vegetable oil
⅓ cup light or dark molasses
2 Tbs. honey
⅓ cup brown sugar
1½ tsp. grated orange rind

1½ cups unbleached all-purpose flour
¾ cup whole-wheat flour
1⅓ cups wheat bran
1 Tbs. baking powder
1½ tsp. baking soda
¼ tsp. salt
¼ tsp. nutmeg or mace

1 cup buttermilk
2 large eggs, lightly beaten
1 tsp. vanilla extract

1. In a small bowl combine raisins and hot water. Set aside to soak and cool.

continued →

Variations
Omit raisins and add
1 cup fresh: strawberries or blueberries or blackberries or chopped peaches or chopped pears or grated apple.
-or-
½ cup dried: apricots or figs or dates.
♥ Use whatever the season makes available ♥

(Bran Muffins, continued)

2. In a small saucepan melt butter, molasses, honey and brown sugar. Add orange rind. Set aside to cool.
3. In a large mixing bowl combine dry ingredients. Mix thoroughly.
4. In a smaller bowl combine buttermilk, eggs, and vanilla. Mix thoroughly. Stir in cooled butter-molasses mixture.
5. Combine wet ingredients and dry ingredients in large mixing bowl. Drain and add raisins. Gently stir just until dry ingredients are moistened. A few lumps may remain - that's OK!
6. Spoon batter into greased muffin tin. Bake in preheated oven for 18-20 minutes or until a toothpick inserted into the middle of muffin comes out clean.

♥ Equally delicious for breakfast, lunch, or dinner ♥

Molasses is a by-product of the sugar-refining process. It's the brownish-black liquid that's left after the sugar crystals have been extracted from sugar cane and sugar beets. Light molasses is produced earlier in the process and is sweeter and lighter in flavor and color. Dark molasses is removed later and is darker, thicker and less sweet. Blackstrap molasses is what's leftover, the dregs, so to speak, and is very dark, very thick, and somewhat bitter in flavor.

Poppyseed Muffins
10 large or 12 medium muffins

More like a little cake than a muffin, it's delicious with any meal. You'll need a mixer to make it - the texture and nice chewy surface depends on thorough mixing of the butter, sugar and eggs.

★ Preheat oven to 350°F. ★ Generously grease muffin tin ★

½ cup butter
1 cup sugar
2 eggs

¾ cup sour cream
1 tsp. vanilla extract
¾ tsp. grated lemon peel

2¼ cups unbleached all-purpose flour
1 tsp. baking powder
¼ tsp. baking soda
¼ cup poppy seeds

1. Combine butter, sugar, and eggs in the electric mixer bowl and beat on medium-high speed for 10 minutes. (Set your timer.)
2. In a small bowl combine dry ingredients, including poppy seeds. Mix thoroughly and set aside.
3. Add sour cream, vanilla, and lemon peel to the butter/sugar mixture in mixer. Mix thoroughly.

continued ⟶

(Poppyseed Muffins, continued)

4. Add dry ingredients in mixer using the lowest speed. Scrape sides of bowl with spatula to combine thoroughly.
5. Spoon batter into prepared muffin tin. Fill 3/4 full to make 12 muffins or to the top to make 10 muffins. Bake in preheated oven for 25-28 minutes or until a toothpick inserted into the middle of muffin comes out clean.

. . . .

notes

Cappuccino Chip Muffins
12 large muffins

This muffin has been included purely for fun! It's not a dinner muffin - although I doubt it would be turned down, if offered. It's made to be enjoyed with a cup of hot coffee, espresso, cappuccino, chocolate, or a tall glass of cold milk!

★ Preheat oven to 350°F. ★ Generously grease muffin tin ★

2 3/4 cups unbleached all-purpose flour
3/4 cup granulated sugar
1 Tbs. instant espresso powder
    or instant coffee powder
2 1/2 tsp. baking powder
1/2 tsp. cinnamon
1/4 tsp. salt
3/4 cup chocolate chips

1 cup milk
2 large eggs, lightly beaten
1 tsp. vanilla extract
1/2 cup melted butter

1. In a large bowl combine dry ingredients, including chocolate chips. Mix thoroughly.
2. In a smaller bowl combine wet ingredients. Mix thoroughly.
3. Combine wet ingredients and dry ingredients in large bowl. Gently stir just until dry ingredients are moistened. A few lumps may remain - that's OK!

continued →

(Cappuccino Chip Muffins, continued)

4. Spoon batter into prepared muffin tin. Bake in preheated oven for 20-23 minutes or until a toothpick inserted into middle of muffin comes out clean.

. . . .

notes 🧁

Savory Garden Muffins
12 large muffins

A great muffin to serve with soup and salad or to enjoy with a chunk of cheese and an apple! Savory (not sweet!), the flavor is reminiscent of Thanksgiving stuffing. Serve warm if possible.

★ Preheat oven to 350° F. ★ generously grease muffin tin ★

- ½ cup butter or vegetable oil
- ½ cup grated carrot
- ¼ cup minced onion
- ¼ cup grated zucchini
- 2 Tbs. <u>each</u> minced red and green bell pepper
- 2 Tbs. minced fresh parsley
- ½ tsp. <u>each</u> thyme and basil

- 2 cups unbleached all-purpose flour
- 1½ cups whole-wheat flour
- 1 Tbs. brown sugar
- 1 Tbs. baking powder
- 1 tsp. baking soda
- 1 tsp. salt

- 2 cups buttermilk
- 2 large eggs, lightly beaten

1. In a medium-sized wide pan or frying pan, sauté veggies and herbs in butter or oil for 5 minutes. Set aside to cool.

continued →

(Savory Garden Muffins, continued)

2. In a large mixing bowl combine dry ingredients. Mix thoroughly.
3. In a smaller bowl combine buttermilk and eggs. Mix thoroughly. Stir in cooled veggie mixture.
4. Combine wet ingredients and dry ingredients in large mixing bowl. Gently stir just until dry ingredients are moistened. A few lumps may remain - that's OK!
5. Spoon batter into greased muffin tin. Bake in preheated oven for 25-30 minutes or until a toothpick inserted in middle of muffin comes out clean.

. . . .
Notes

Mexican Corn Muffins
12 large muffins

A delicious little meal-in-a-muffin. These muffins keep well and are handy to take on the road. Great with Robert's Chili, Mexi-Corn Chowder, and Mexi-Cali Rice.

★ Preheat oven to 350°F. ★ Generously grease muffin tin ★

¼ cup butter or vegetable oil
2 Tbs <u>each</u> minced onion, minced fresh parsley, minced red and green bell pepper
½ cup fresh or frozen corn
1 Tbs. salsa

1½ cups unbleached all-purpose flour
1½ cups yellow cornmeal
¼ cup brown sugar
2 tsp. baking powder
¾ tsp. baking soda
¾ tsp. salt
¾ cup shredded Cheddar cheese

1½ cups buttermilk
2 large eggs, lightly beaten

1. In a medium-sized wide pan or frying pan sauté veggies in butter or oil for 5 minutes. Add salsa and set aside to cool.
2. In a large mixing bowl combine dry ingredients including cheese. Mix thoroughly.

continued ⟶

(Mexican Corn Muffins, continued)

3. In a smaller bowl combine buttermilk and eggs. Mix thoroughly. Stir in cooled veggie mixture.
4. Combine wet ingredients and dry ingredients in large mixing bowl. Gently stir just until dry ingredients are moistened. A few lumps may remain — that's OK!
5. Spoon batter into greased muffin tin. Bake in preheated oven for 22-25 minutes or until a toothpick inserted into the middle of muffin comes out clean.

. . . .

Notes ♥

Gingerbread
9 inch square or round pan

This is the <u>best</u> gingerbread! It's tremendous with many of the soups and salads. Serve it warm from the oven with Old Fashioned Turkey Barley Soup, Nutty Brown Rice and sharp Cheddar cheese, served on a cutting board, to slice as you eat.

★ Preheat oven to 350°F. ★ Grease and flour baking pan ★
note: You'll need an electric mixer.

1 cup water
2/3 cup light or dark molasses
1/2 cup butter

2 1/2 cups unbleached all-purpose flour
1 1/2 tsp. baking soda
1/2 tsp. baking powder
2 tsp. ginger
1 tsp. cinnamon
1/2 tsp. cloves
1/2 tsp. nutmeg
1/4 tsp. salt
1/2 cup finely-chopped crystallized ginger, optional

3/4 cup brown sugar
2 eggs

1. In small saucepan heat water, molasses, and butter over low heat until butter melts. Set aside to cool.

continued →

(Gingerbread, continued)

2. In a large bowl combine dry ingredients, including crystallized ginger if you have some to use (I hope you do; it makes this excellent gingerbread even better)! Mix thoroughly.
3. Combine brown sugar and eggs in the electric mixer bowl and beat on medium-high speed until thick, creamy, and light.
4. Alternately add cooled molasses mixture and dry ingredients to the brown sugar/egg mixture. Use the lowest speed and mix thoroughly, scraping the sides and bottom of bowl between additions.
5. Spread batter into baking pan. Bake in preheated oven for 40-45 minutes. Or until a toothpick inserted in the center comes out clean.

Serving Suggestion: Delicious ways to serve gingerbread:
- ♥ With a dollop of fresh whipped cream.
- ♥ With a chunk of sharp Cheddar and an apple.
- ♥ With a cup of hot Irish Breakfast tea and an orange.
- ♥ With a Café Latté - get one "to go" at the Café.
- ♥ You can even frost it with Cream Cheese frosting... and serve it for dessert!

Notes ♥

Buttermilk Oatmeal Bread
2 loaves

This is a yeast bread that you will want to make over and over again. I know, I've been making it for almost 20 years. Yes, this is the bread I learned on, and although it's changed a little over the years (what hasn't?), it's still just as easy to make and even more delicious to eat.

2 packages dry yeast
1 tsp. sugar or honey
¼ cup warm (100°) water

2 cups buttermilk
¼ cup molasses
¼ cup brown sugar or honey
1 cup old-fashioned oatmeal
1 cup unbleached bread flour

1½ tsp. salt
¼ cup melted butter or vegetable oil

1 cup whole-wheat flour
3-4 cups unbleached bread flour

1. In a small bowl combine sugar and yeast with warm water. Let it "proof" (the yeast becomes foamy and "proves" it's alive) in a warm draft-free place for 5 minutes.

continued ⟶

(Buttermilk Oatmeal Bread, continued)

2. In a small saucepan combine buttermilk, molasses, and brown sugar and warm over low heat. (Have a microwave? "Wave it" for 75 seconds.) You are just taking the chill off to keep the yeast happy.
3. In a large mixing bowl combine the yeast mixture, buttermilk mixture, oatmeal, and first cup of flour. By hand, stir 150 strong strokes. (If you have a bread-making mixer do this in the mixing bowl, beating with the flat beater for 2 minutes on medium speed.) This is called the "sponge." Cover bowl with a clean towel or plastic wrap and let rise for 30 minutes in a warm place. It will become nice and bubbly.
4. Stir in the butter or oil and salt. Gradually add the rest of the flour, starting with the whole-wheat. Stir until the dough starts to pull away from the sides of the bowl and forms a rough ball. Turn the dough out onto a lightly floured surface, and knead by hand, adding more flour, a little at a time, until it is no longer sticky and you have a smooth, satiny ball of dough. This takes 10-15 minutes. (If you are using a bread-making mixer add the flour, and using the dough-hook attachment, mix 4-5 minutes.)
5. Transfer the dough to a large, lightly oiled bowl and place in a warm, draft-free spot. Cover the bowl and let rise until doubled in size, 45 minutes to 1 hour.
6. Punch down the risen dough, turn out onto a lightly-floured work surface, and let rest, covered, for 10 minutes.

continued ⟶

(Buttermilk Oatmeal Bread, continued)

7. Prepare your pans by lightly greasing and then sprinkling with a little oatmeal. To make 2 9-inch sandwich-size bread loaves, divide the dough into 2 pieces, shape into loaves, and push into prepared pans. Push the dough into the corners. (You can also form the dough into many exciting bread shapes like braids, ovals, long loaves, knots, and swirls, so be creative here - if you want to!) Sprinkle a little more oatmeal on top of the loaf and press it in a bit. This will give you a crunchier crust. If you want a chewy, shiny crust, brush the top with "eggwash" (one egg beaten with 1 Tbs. water). For a soft crust, brush with melted butter.
8. Place loaves in a warm, draft-free spot and let rise again until doubled and risen dough is well above the top edge of the pan, about 30-40 minutes.
9. Preheat oven to 350°F, 20 minutes before baking bread.
10. Bake the loaves until they are a lovely golden-brown. Turn one out from its pan. It will feel light and, when patted on the bottom, sound hollow when it is done. If not, return to the oven for 5-10 more minutes. The loaves will take approximately 40 minutes to bake. (Smaller loaves and rolls will take less time to bake, so check accordingly.) When done, remove from the oven, turn from the pans, and place on a metal rack to cool before slicing.

Café Cornbread
one 9 inch square or round pan
6-8 servings

We serve this cornbread almost daily through the winter months with our home-made soups. A delicious easy-to-make cornbread!

★ Preheat oven to 375°F. ★ Grease and flour baking pan ★

1/4 cup butter
1/4 cup brown sugar

1 1/2 cups unbleached all-purpose flour
1 cup yellow cornmeal
2 1/2 tsp. baking powder
3/4 tsp. baking soda
3/4 tsp. salt

1/2 cup buttermilk
2/3 cup milk
1 large egg, lightly beaten

1. In a small saucepan melt butter and brown sugar. Set aside to cool.
2. In a large mixing bowl combine dry ingredients. Mix thoroughly.
3. In a smaller bowl combine buttermilk, milk, and egg. Mix thoroughly. Stir in cooled butter-sugar mixture.
4. Combine wet ingredients and dry ingredients in large mixing bowl. Gently stir just until dry ingredients are moistened. A few lumps may remain — that's OK!
5. Spread batter into baking pan. Bake in preheated oven for 25-30 minutes or until toothpick comes out clean.

Irish Soda Bread
2 round loaves

A favorite of mine, I make it every St. Patrick's day and as often as possible in between. Very easy, very pretty, very good. It's especially delicious toasted with butter and jam on it. Or take it on a picnic and eat hand-torn pieces with cheese and fruit. "A darling of a bread" – thanks to the Irish!

★ Preheat oven to 350°F. ★ Lightly grease cookie sheet ★

¼ cup butter or vegetable oil
¼ cup brown sugar

3 cups unbleached all-purpose flour
¾ cup old-fashioned oatmeal
1 tsp. salt
1½ tsp. baking powder
1 tsp. baking soda
½ cup raisins

1 cup buttermilk
1 large egg, lightly beaten

> ♧ Variations ♧
> Feel free to experiment.
> Try dried fruit or chopped nuts or grated apple instead of raisins.
> "Erin go bragh!"

1. In a small saucepan melt butter and brown sugar. Set aside to cool.
2. In a large mixing bowl combine dry ingredients including raisins. Mix thoroughly.
3. In a smaller bowl combine buttermilk and egg. Mix thoroughly. Stir in cooled butter-sugar mixture.

continued →

(Irish Soda Bread, continued)

4. Combine wet ingredients and dry ingredients. Gently stir until thoroughly mixed. The mixture will form a ball.
5. Turn ball of dough out onto a lightly-floured surface (a clean countertop will do). Knead with your hands a few times. Divide into 2 equal pieces and form into 2 round loaves. Flatten loaves to about 1½" thick.
6. Transfer the loaves to the prepared cookie sheet and make the traditional cross-cut in the top of each loaf with a sharp knife - a "✛" ½" deep. Bake in preheated oven for 35-40 minutes or until the loaves are a lovely golden brown and sound hollow when tapped on the bottom.

. . . .

Notes:

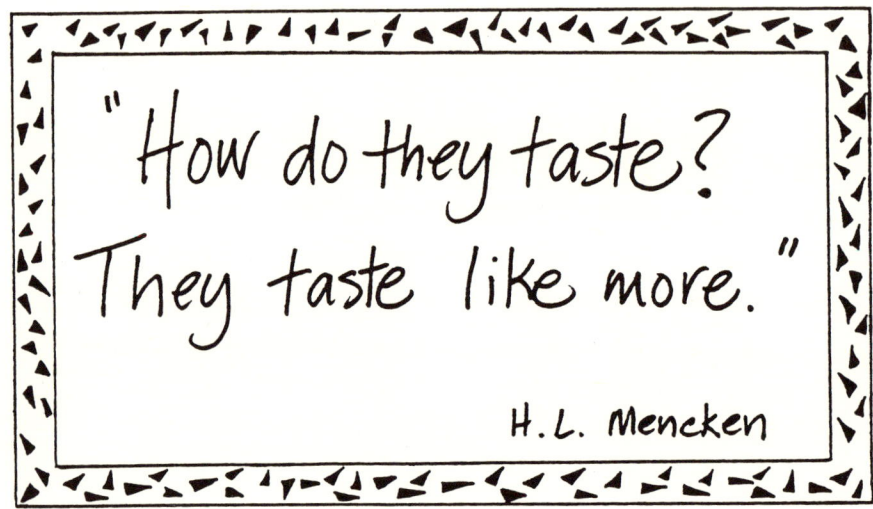

"How do they taste?
They taste like more."

— H.L. Mencken

Two absolutely excellent entrées that insisted on being included

 Chicken Pasties

 Café Pizza

Chicken Pasties (páss-tees)
4 servings

Delicious served with a fresh green salad and some applesauce. A comfort meal without a doubt! To save yourself time in the evening, make and roll out the pastry the night before or in the morning. Wrap well and refrigerate until ready.

♥ note to vegetarians: You can easily make this recipe meatfree! Substitute tofu for the chicken and water for the chicken broth... Equally delicious!

The Pastry

1 recipe quiche pastry (p.114)

Prepare pastry as instructed through Step 3 on pgs. 114-115. Divide into 4 pieces and form into round balls. On a lightly floured surface, flatten one ball and sprinkle with flour. Roll out with a rolling pin to form a circle 10" wide. Brush off excess flour. Roll out the remaining balls of pastry and place on a plate with pieces of wax paper between each circle of pastry, cover well, and refrigerate until ready to use.

The Chicken

2 cups water
1/4 tsp. salt
3/4 lb. skinless boneless chicken breast, (about 3 chicken breast halves.)

continued →

(Chicken Pasties, continued)

Heat water to a low simmer. Add salt and chicken. Simmer, covered, until the chicken is firm to the touch, 10-15 minutes. Remove chicken and reserve broth for the filling. Cool slightly and cut chicken into bite-sized pieces. Set aside.

The Filling

- 1 Tbs. butter or vegetable oil
- 1/2 tsp. salt
- 1 cup chopped onions
- 1/2 cup sliced carrots
- 1/2 cup sliced celery
- 1 cup peeled and diced potatoes
- 1 cup sliced fresh mushrooms

- 1/4 tsp. each tarragon and marjoram
- 1/4 tsp. black pepper
- 1/8 tsp. dill weed
- 3/4 cup reserved chicken broth

- 1 1/2 Tbs. flour
- cooked chicken
- 1/4 cup sour cream

1. In large frying pan sauté veggies with salt for 5 minutes. Cover and cook 5-7 minutes more, until veggies are tender. (Stir often—the potatoes have a tendency to stick.)

continued ⟶

(Chicken Pasties, continued)

2. Stir in herbs and spices. Add chicken broth and bring to a simmer. Add flour, a little at a time, and stir until thick and bubbly, 1-2 minutes.
3. Stir in chicken pieces and sour cream. Remove from heat. Cool for 10 minutes. (Now's a good time to sip wine!)
4. Preheat oven to 375°F. Lightly grease a cookie sheet.

The Finale

1. Remove pastry circles from the refrigerator and place on a clean, flat surface. (Cutting board or counter work fine.) With your eyes, divide the circle in half. Make a little mark to show where the center line is. Above the center line, in the top half of the circle, make 3 1-inch slashes with a sharp knife or pizza cutter. Below the center line, in the middle of the bottom half, place a heaping ½ cup of the filling, leaving a ½-inch rim along the edge. Fold the top half over the bottom half. Tuck the bottom rim over the top to seal and pinch into a fluted edge or crimp with a fork.

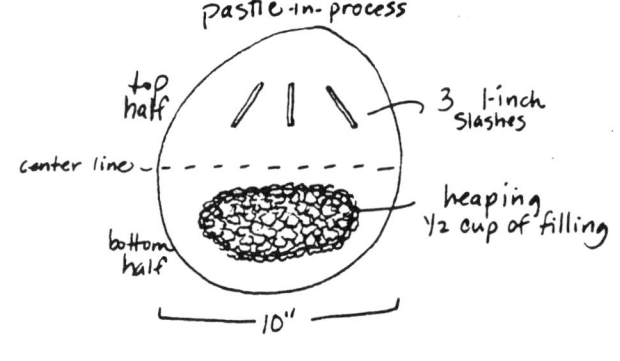

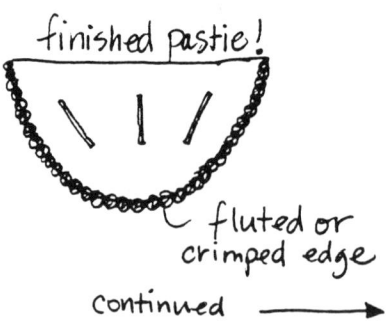

continued →

(Chicken Pasties, continued)

2. Place completed pastie on the prepared cookie sheet. Finish remaining pasties and place on the sheet pan. Bake in preheated oven for 25-35 minutes, until the crust is a light golden brown and the filling is hot and bubbly.

· ·

Notes 🍲

Café Pizza

Our own deluxe pizza! This recipe makes 2 12x15-inch pizzas <u>or</u> 2 16-inch round pizzas <u>or</u> 24 4 to 5-inch round personal pizzas <u>or</u> 36 3-inch round mini-pizzas.

> ★note: there are so many different sizes of pans that it can cause confusion. It need not - pizza is a forgiving food that has no trouble altering its shape to fit your pan size. My pizza pan measures 12"x15", but any size close to those dimensions can be used for this recipe. One word of caution: don't use too small a pan. The dough should be as thin as possible to create a crispy, chewy crust that is not bready.

Each of the larger pizzas will feed 3 to 4 hungry people when accompanied by a fresh salad. So a full recipe makes 2 pizzas and will feed 6 to 8. If you don't need that much pizza (don't forget to plan ahead for leftovers to eat cold the next day - one of life's little pleasures...), you can freeze half the dough and sauce to use later. After completing the dough (before letting it rise), divide it equally in half. Put the half you are going to use now aside to do its rising and the other half in a 1 to 2 lb. oiled plastic container (like cottage or ricotta cheese comes in). Cover tightly and freeze. It will keep for several weeks in the freezer and defrosts in 3 hours at room temperature or 6 hours in the refrigerator. Follow the same process for the sauce, letting it cool a little before filling the containers. The sauce will take the same amount of time to thaw.

continued ⟶

(Café Pizza, continued)

What you now have is a freshly-made pizza dinner that you can prepare and serve within a half-hour. Just transfer the sauce and dough from freezer to refrigerator in the morning. It'll be ready for you to put together in the afternoon. Quite a treat on a busy work day... Enjoy!

A word about <u>pizza stones</u> — I love using mine! You really do get a crisper, chewier crust. A pizza stone is simply a flat piece of unglazed clay that produces a dry heat which absorbs moisture when you bake on it. The result is a crust that is nicely browned and crisp on the outside but still chewy and good on the inside. The stone doubles as a serving platter and keeps your pizza warm throughout the meal.

Personal pizzas and mini-pizzas — Personal pizzas are great for parties-for kids and adults alike! Mini-pizzas make wonderful appetizers to take to a pot-luck or serve on a buffet. Here's how you do it: divide the pizza dough into 24 pieces for personal pizzas and 36 pieces for mini-pizzas. Roll into little balls and let rest 5 minutes. With a rolling pin or your hands, flatten each ball into a circle 5 inches wide for personal pizzas and 3 inches wide for mini-pizzas. Top with the sauce and toppings of your choice and bake in a 450°F preheated oven for 10 to 15 minutes.

continued ⟶

(Café Pizza, continued)

The Dough - enough for 2 pizzas

- 1¼ cup. warm (100°) water
- 1 tsp. honey
- 1 package active dry yeast
- 2 Tbs. olive oil
- 2½ to 3 cups unbleached all-purpose flour
- ½ cup whole-wheat flour
- 1 tsp. salt

1. Combine water, honey, yeast, and olive oil in a large bowl. Mix well. Stir in 2 cups unbleached flour and salt and beat with a large wooden spoon for 2 minutes. Add the remaining flour, starting with the whole-wheat, ½ cup at a time, stirring until the dough forms a ball.
2. Turn the dough out onto a lightly-floured surface and knead until it is smooth and elastic, about 8 to 10 minutes. (If the dough becomes sticky while you are kneading it, sprinkle on a little more flour and continue to knead.)
3. Transfer the dough to a large lightly-oiled bowl. Cover with plastic wrap or a clean towel and let rise until doubled in size, about 1 hour.
   - ♥ note: prepare sauce and toppings while the dough rises.
4. When the dough has risen, uncover and gently push down. Divide the dough evenly in half for 2 pizzas. Cover dough with a towel and let rest a few minutes before placing it on the pan and forming the crust. If you're going to make small

continued →

(Café Pizza, continued)

pizzas, follow directions for personal pizzas and mini-pizzas on previous page.) Place half of the dough in the center of your lightly-oiled pizza pan and press evenly towards the edge forming the crust. It will be thin — that's right! Make a slightly thicker rim of dough along the outside edge to hold the toppings on. Repeat with other half of dough if you're making 2 pizzas.

5. Drizzle 1 Tbs. olive oil on top of crust and spread around with your fingers.

The Chunky Tomato Sauce - enough for 2 pizzas

- 2 Tbs. olive oil
- 2-3 large cloves garlic, minced
- 1 cup chopped onions
- 1/2 cup sliced celery
- 1/4 cup minced fresh parsley
- 1 14 1/2-oz. can diced tomatoes in puree
- 2 Tbs. tomato paste
- 1 tsp. basil
- 1/2 tsp. oregano or marjoram
- 1/2 tsp. thyme
- 1/4 tsp. black pepper
- 1/4 tsp. salt, more to taste

Heat olive oil in a large frying pan or wide saucepan. Add garlic and brown slightly. Add onions, celery and parsley; sauté until tender, 5 to 7 minutes. Add canned tomatoes, tomato paste, herbs, and seasonings; cook uncovered for 15 minutes, stirring occasionally. The sauce will be thick and quite chunky when done.

continued →

(Café Pizza, continued)

This is enough sauce for 2 large pizzas. If you are freezing half, divide into 1-cup amounts. Freeze 1 cup in a clean plastic container with a tight lid. Set aside the remaining cup to use when you build your pizza.

The Toppings - enough for 2 pizzas

- 2 cups chunky tomato sauce (p. 171)
- 1/4 to 1/2 cup pesto (p. 32)
- 2 Tbs. chopped fresh parsley
- 1 cup sliced fresh mushrooms
- 1/2 cup black olives, quartered lengthwise
- 1/4 cup sliced green onions
- 1 6-oz jar sliced artichoke hearts, drained
- 1-2 cups shredded mozzarella cheese
- 1/2 cup shredded Cheddar cheese
- 1/4 cup grated Parmesan cheese

These are the toppings that adorn our Café Pizza. I think they are delicious and well-balanced, but tastes differ. Please feel free to use any or all of the toppings or choose a few of your own favorites. You are making the pizza - use a little artistic license!

★note: These are enough topping ingredients for 2 large pizzas. If you are going to freeze half of the dough and sauce as discussed earlier, prepare only half the amount of toppings to make one pizza.

continued ⟶

(Café Pizza, continued)

The Construction (Building a Café Pizza)

Have ready:
- 1 or 2 pizza pans covered with dough
- Chunky tomato sauce
- Assorted prepared toppings

On top of crust (and all the way to the edge)
1. Spread the pesto evenly across.
2. Spread the chunky tomato sauce on top of pesto.
3. Sprinkle chopped parsley.
4. Evenly distribute sliced mushrooms.
5. Scatter the green onions.
6. Sprinkle on the black olives.
7. Evenly distribute the drained artichoke hearts.
8. Cover with shredded mozzarella cheese.
9. Sprinkle with shredded Cheddar cheese.
10. Finally, top with grated Parmesan cheese.

Take a good look - a feast for the eyes! Place in the preheated 450°F. oven and bake until the crust and cheese are a light golden brown, 10-15 minutes.

. . . .

notes
♥ and ♥
new ideas

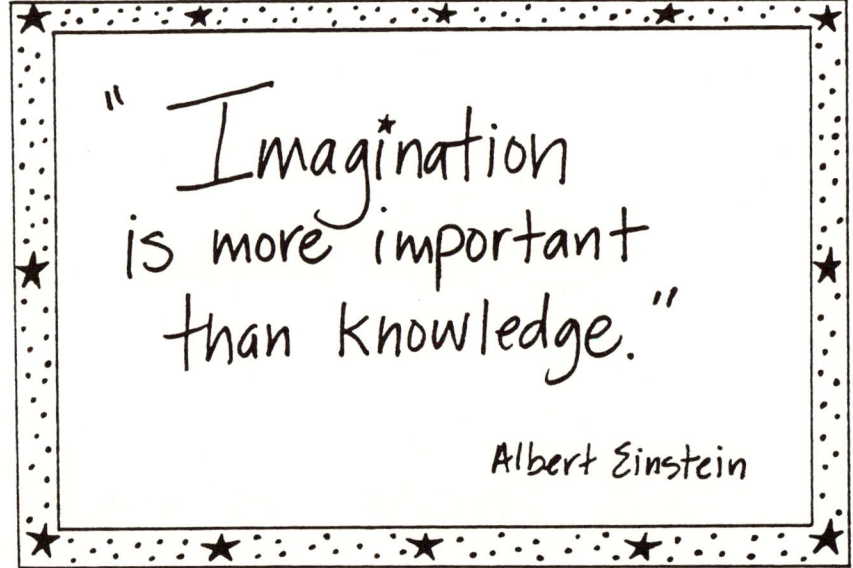

"Imagination is more important than knowledge."

Albert Einstein

Epilogue

Sigh... Upon finishing this cookbook I marvel at the fact that I'm actually done. This has been an incredibly good experience - so enjoyable to be totally focused on a project with a minimum of interruptions. (Yes - I worked at home!) Although the phone was by my side to answer my crews' questions and a few catastrophes brought me back into the Café for awhile, I mainly worked on this book for the last 9 months. I had no idea of the complexity of this project when I began (not an unusual happening in my life). But it is just that complexity, the total immersion necessary to reach completion, that made the experience so rich.

    I've missed the Café and all my customers (many of whom are now friends) and I look forward to seeing you all again. My thanks to everyone involved in helping this happen and giving me the opportunity to share with those interested in what I love doing.

A rabbi spoke with the Lord about Heaven and Hell. "I will show you Hell," said the Lord and they went into a room which had a large pot of stew in the middle. The smell was delicious and around the pot sat people who were famished and desperate. All were holding spoons with very long handles which reached to the pot, but because the handles of the spoons were longer than their arms, it was impossible to get the stew back into their mouths. Their suffering was terrible.

"Now I will show you Heaven," said the Lord, and they went into an identical room. There was the same pot of stew and the people had the same identical spoons, but they were well-nourished, talking, and happy. At first the rabbi did not understand. "It is simple," said the Lord. "You see, they have learned to feed each other."

Jewish parable

Index

A

a la Greek pasta salad, 89
albacore tuna pasta salad, 92
antipasto pasta salad, 74
apple cider vinegar, about, 18
ARTICHOKES, in...
  a la Greek pasta, 89
  antipasto pasta salad, 74
  Cafe pizza, 168
  garden veggie pasta, 88
  quiche, 131
  San Francisco rice, 104
  Sicilian quiche, 130
asparagus & ham quiche, 131
autumn vegetable quiche, 124

B

baker's yeast, about, 138
BAKING,
  basics, 135
  powder, about, 137
  powder, to make, 138
  soda, about, 136
Balsamic vinegar, about, 18
barbecue, about, 71
BARLEY, in...
  country vegetable
    soup, 42
  old-fashioned turkey
    soup, 54
BASIL,
  about. 90
  in...
    fresh tomato Parmesan, 90
    herb vinegar, 18
    pesto, 32
BEANS,
  garbanzo, in...
    chicken couscous salad, 94
    quick hummus, 93
  lentil soup, 43
  pinto, in Robert's chili, 39
  red, in minestrone soup, 46
  white, in...
    minestrone soup, 46
    U.S. Senate bean soup, 50
blue cheese dressing, 30
Brie quiche, 131

Index

bran muffins, 144
BREADS AND MUFFINS, 133-161
   about, 134
   baking basics, 135
   bran muffins, 144
   buttermilk oatmeal bread, 156
   Cafe cornbread, 159
   Cafe pizza, dough for, 170
   cappuccino chip muffins, 148
   cranberry-orange muffins, 140
   gingerbread, 154
   Irish soda bread, 160
   leavening agents for, 136
   lemon-pecan muffins, 142
   Mexican corn muffins, 152
   poppyseed muffins, 146
   quiche pastry, 114
   savory garden muffins, 150
BROCCOLI,
   Cheddar soup, 44
   -Cheddar quiche, 119
   and ham quiche, 131
   fresh herbs, and
     cheeses quiche, 120
brown rice salad, nutty, 96
BUTTERMILK, in...
     bran muffins, 144
     Irish soda bread, 160
     Mexican corn muffins, 152
     savory garden muffins, 150
     -oatmeal bread, 156

C

Cafe cornbread, 159
Cafe pizza, 168
canola oil, about, 20
cappuccino chip muffins, 148
cauliflower, in soup, 44
CHEESE,
   and onion pie, 117
   blue cheese dressing, 30
   Brie quiche, 131
   Cheddar, in...
     broccoli soup, 44
     potato soup, 58
     Santa Fe soup, 60
     turkey quiche, 131
   cream cheese, in...
     broccoli, fresh herbs and
       cheeses quiche, 120
     creamy Italian dressing, 27
   Feta, in...
     Greek quiche, 131
     pasta a la Greek, 89
   jack, in Teriyaki chicken
     quiche, 131
   mozzarella, in Cafe
     pizza topping, 172
   Parmesan, in...
     garlic butter, 43
     fresh tomato pasta, 90
     pesto, 32
     vinaigrette dressing, 26
   provolone, in antipasto
     pasta salad, 74
   ricotta, in spinach ricotta
     pie, 126
   Swiss, in quiches, 107-131
CHICKEN,
   couscous salad, 94
   pasties, 164
   Szechuan salad, 86
   Teriyaki, 70
    in...
     couscous salad, 94
     Oriental sesame pasta
       salad, 85
     sesame rice salad, 102
     spinach pasta salad, 76
     Szechuan pasta salad, 86
     Thai pasta salad, 78
   sauce for, 33
CHILI,
   powder, about, 41
   Robert's, 39
chunky tomato sauce, 171

Index

cilantro, about, 87
CORN,
  -bread, Cafe, 159
  in...
    Mexican muffins, 152
    Mexi-corn chowder, 56
    Robert's chili, 39
    savory muffins, 150
  oil, about, 20
country vegetable barley
  soup, 42
COUSCOUS,
  about, 95
  for breakfast, 95
  salad, chicken, 94
cranberry-orange muffins, 140
cream cheese, in...
  broccoli, fresh herbs and
    cheeses quiche, 120
  creamy Italian dressing, 27
cream of tartar, about, 137
creamy Italian dressing, 27
create a quiche, 131
crust for a quiche, 110, 114
curry powder, about, 97
custard for quiche, 112, 116

D

DRESSINGS, 15-33
  about, 17
  blue cheese, 30
  for chicken couscous
    salad, 94
  creamy Italian, 27
  fruit vinegars, 19
  garlic, in, 22
  ginger root, in, 24
  herbs, in, 23
  herb vinegars, 18

  honey mustard, 29
  for Leslie's zingy potato
    salad, 105
  marinades, 25, 28, 33
  mayonnaise,
    -dressed salads, 69
    in turkey pasta salad, 80
  mustard, in, 23
  for Mexi-Cali rice
    salad, 98
  for nutty brown rice
    salad, 96
  oils for, 19
  Oriental, 28
  Parmesan vinaigrette, 26
  pesto, 32
  for San Francisco rice
    salad, 104
  for sesame chicken rice
    salad, 102
  for smoked turkey rice
    salad, 100
  soy sauce, in, 24
  for spinach-chicken pasta
    salad, 76
  sweet hot mustard, 31
  Teriyaki sauce, 33
  for Thai chicken pasta
    salad, 78
  vinaigrette dressing, 25
  vinegar, in, 17

F

FETA CHEESE, in...
  pasta a la Greek
    salad, 89
  Greek quiche, 131
fresh tomato Parmesan pasta
  salad, 90
fruit vinegars, about, 19

Index

G

GARBANZO BEANS, in...
  chicken couscous salad, 94
  quick hummus, 93
garden veggie pasta salad, 88
GARLIC,
  about, 22
  -Parmesan butter, 43
ginger root, about, 24
gingerbread, 154
Greek quiche, 131

H

HAM, in...
  antipasto salad, 74
  quiches, 131
  quiche Lorraine, 125
  Sicilian quiche, 130
  U.S. Senate bean soup, 50
HERBS,
  about, 23, 67
  basil, 23, 32, 90
  cilantro, 87
  fresh, in quiche, 120
  substituting fresh for
    dry, 23, 67
  tarragon, 55
  in vinegars, 18
honey mustard dressing, 29
hot oil, about, 20
HOW TO...
  cook pasta perfectly, 68
  create a quiche, 131
  dress pasta with mayo, 69
  heat milk-based soups, 38
  prepare perfect quiche, 109
  prepare Teriyaki chicken, 70
hummus, quick, 93

I

Irish soda bread, 160

J

jack cheese, see 131
JALAPENO PEPPERS,
  about, 79
  in...
    Mexi-Cali rice salad, 98
    Mexi-corn chowder, 56
    Robert's chili, 39
    Santa Fe Cheddar soup, 60
    Thai chicken pasta
      salad, 78

L

leavening agents, about, 136
LEMON,
  juice, about, 22
  -pecan muffins, 142
  zest, about, 141
lentil soup, 48
Leslie's zingy potato
  salad, 105
Lorraine, quiche, 125

M

malt vinegar, about, 18
MARINADES, see also
  DRESSINGS,
  about, 17
  Oriental dressing, 28
  Teriyaki sauce, 33
  vinaigrette dressing, 25
MAYONNAISE,
  in turkey pasta salad, 80

Index

    to dress pasta with, 69
MEAT-FREE DISHES,
  Cafe pizza, 168
  hints for, 95
  salads,
    fresh tomato Parmesan, 90
    garden veggie pasta, 88
    Leslie's zingy potato, 105
    Mexi-Cali rice, 98
    nutty brown rice, 96
    Oriental sesame pasta, 85
    pasta a la Greek, 89
    pesto pasta, 73
    ricotta tortellini, 84
    San Francisco rice, 104
  soups,
    broccoli Cheddar, 44
    country vegetable barley, 42
    lentil, 48
    Mexi-corn chowder, 56
    minestrone, 46
    potato Cheddar, 58
    Robert's chili, 39
    Santa Fe Cheddar, 69
    tomato tortellini, 52
  quiches,
    autumn vegetable, 124
    broccoli-Cheddar, 119
    broccoli, fresh herbs, and cheeses, 120
    cheese and onion pie, 117
    ideas for, 131
    savory mushroom, 118
    savory squash pie, 128
    spinach ricotta pie, 126
    Spanish, 122
Mexican corn muffins, 152
Mexi-Cali rice salad, 98
Mexi-corn chowder, 56
milk-based soups, about, 38
minestrone soup, 46
molasses, about, 144
mostaccioli, see PASTA
mozzarella, in Cafe pizza topping, 172

MUFFINS AND BREADS, 133-161
  about, 134
  baking basics, 135
  bran muffins, 144
  buttermilk oatmeal bread, 156
  Cafe cornbread, 159
  cappuccino chip muffins, 148
  cranberry-orange muffins, 140
  gingerbread, 154
  Irish soda bread, 160
  leavening agents for, 136
  lemon-pecan muffins, 142
  Mexican corn muffins, 152
  poppyseed muffins, 146
  savory garden muffins, 150
mushroom quiche, savory, 118
MUSTARD,
  about, 23
  and honey dressing, 29
  sweet hot dressing, 31

N

nutty brown rice salad, 96

O

oatmeal buttermilk bread, 156
OILS,
  about, 19-21
  canola, 20
  corn, 20
  hot, 20
  olive, 21
  peanut, 20
  sesame, 20
  sesame, Oriental, 20, 28
  soy, 20
  sunflower, 20
  walnut, 20
old-fashioned turkey barley soup, 54

Index

olive oil, about, 21
orange zest, about, 141
Oregon shrimp pasta salad, 91
ORIENTAL,
  dressing, 28
    in...
      chicken Szechuan pasta
        salad, 86
      sesame pasta salad, 85
  sesame oil, about, 20, 28
  sesame pasta salad, 85

P

PARMESAN, in...
  fresh tomato salad, 90
  garlic butter, 43
  pesto, 32
  vinaigrette dressing, 26
PASTA, 64-92
  about, 68
  bow ties, in...
    Oregon shrimp salad, 91
    Oriental sesame salad, 85
    Thai chicken salad, 78
  illustrated, 69
  mostaccioli, in...
    albacore tuna salad, 92
    pasta a la Greek salad, 89
  rotini (spiral)
    in...
      chicken Szechuan salad, 86
      fresh tomato Parmesan
        salad, 90
      pesto pasta salad, 73
    rainbow, in garden veggie
      pasta salad, 88
  salads,
    about, 64
    a la Greek, 89
    albacore tuna, 92
    antipasto, 74
    chicken Szechuan, 86
    garden veggie, 88
    mayo dressed, 69
    Oregon shrimp, 91
    Oriental sesame, 85
    pesto, 73
    riccota tortellini, 84
    spinach-chicken, 76
    Thai chicken, 78
    turkey tortellini, 82
    turkey mayo, 80
  shell, in...
    antipasto, 74
    spinach-chicken salad, 76
    turkey mayo salad, 80
  spiral, see PASTA, rotini.
  soups,
    tomato tortellini, 52
  tortellini,
    about, 53
    in...
      ricotta salad, 84
      tomato soup, 52
      turkey salad, 82
pasta a la Greek salad, 89
pasties, chicken, 164
pastry for quiche, 110, 114
peanut oil, about, 20
pecan and lemon muffins, 142
pepper, black, about, 29
peppers, hot, see JALAPENOS
pesto pasta salad, 73
PESTO,
  in...
    Cafe pizza, 172
    pesto pasta salad, 73
  sauce, 32
pine nuts, 32
pizza, Cafe, 168
poppyseed muffins, 146
potato Cheddar soup, 58
potato salad, Leslie's zingy, 105
provolone cheese, in
  Antipasto pasta salad, 74
pumpkin, in quiche, 128

Index

Q

QUICHES, 107-131
  about, 109-113
  artichoke, 131
  asparagus, fresh, 131
  autumn vegetable, 124
  Brie, 131
  broccoli-Cheddar, 119
  broccoli, fresh herbs and
    cheeses, 120
  cheese and onion pie, 117
  create a, 131
  custard for, 116
  Greek, 131
  ham, 131
  Lorraine, 125
  pastry for, 110, 114
  savory mushroom, 118
  savory squash pie, 128
  Sicilian, 130
  Spanish, 122
  spinach ricotta pie, 126
  teriyaki chicken, 131
  turkey and Cheddar, 131
quick hummus, 92

R

RICE,
  brown, in...
    Mexi-Cali rice salad, 98
    nutty brown rice
      salad, 96
    sesame chicken rice
      salad, 102
    smoked turkey wild rice
      salad, 10
  wild,
    about, 103
    in...
      sesame chicken salad, 102
      smoked turkey salad, 100
    white, in San Francisco
      salad, 104
rice vinegar, about, 18, 103
ricotta tortellini salad, 84
ricotta cheese, in spinach
  pie, 126
Robert's chili, 39
rotini, see PASTA

S

salmon, smoked, in rice
  salad, see 101
SALADS, 64-105
  about, 64-67
  albacore tuna pasta, 92
  antipasto pasta, 74
  chicken couscous, 94
  chicken Szechuan pasta, 86
  fresh tomato Parmesan, 90
  garden veggie pasta, 88
  Leslie's zingy potato, 105
  Mexi-Cali rice, 98
  nutty brown rice, 96
  Oregon shrimp pasta, 91
  Oriental sesame pasta, 85
  pasta a la Greek, 89
  pesto pasta, 73
  ricotta tortellini, 84
  San Francisco rice, 104
  sesame chicken rice, 102
  smoked turkey wild rice, 100
  spinach-chicken pasta, 76
  Thai chicken pasta, 78
  turkey pasta mayo, 80
  turkey tortellini, 82
San Francisco rice salad, 104
Santa Fe Cheddar soup, 60
savory garden muffins, 150
savory mushroom quiche, 118
savory squash pie, 128

Index

SESAME,
  chicken rice salad, 102
  oil,
    about, 20
    Oriental, about, 20, 28
  pasta salad, Oriental, 85
Sicilian quiche, 130
smoked turkey wild rice
  salad, 100
SOUPS, 35-61
  about, 36-38
  Cheddar broccoli, 44
  country vegetable barley, 42
  lentil, 48
  Mexi-corn chowder, 56
  milk-based, about, 38
  minestrone, 46
  old-fashioned turkey
    barley, 54
  potato Cheddar, 59
  Robert's chili, 39
  Santa Fe Cheddar, 60
  tomato tortellini, 52
  U.S. Senate bean, 50
soy oil, about, 20
soy sauce, about, 24
Spanish quiche, 122
spinach-chicken pasta, 76
spinach ricotta pie, 126
squash, winter, in savory
  pie, 128
sunflower oil, about, 20
sweet-hot mustard dressing, 31
Swiss cheese in
    quiches, 107-131

T

tamari, about 33
tarragon, about, 55
TERIYAKI,
  chicken, 70
    in...
      chicken salad,
        Szechuan, 86
      Oriental sesame pasta
        salad, 85
      sesame chicken rice
        salad, 102
      Thai chicken pasta
        salad, 78
      quiche, 131
  sauce, 33
    in...
      Oriental marinade, 28
      sesame chicken rice
        salad, 102
Thai chicken pasta, 78
tofu, marinated, 72
tomato sauce for Cafe
  pizza, 171
tomato tortellini soup, 52
TOMATOES, FRESH, in...
  antipasto pasta salad, 74
  chicken couscous salad, 94
  garden veggie pasta salad, 88
  Mexi-Cali rice salad, 98
  minestrone soup, 46
  Parmesan salad, 90
  pesto pasta salad, 73
  ricotta tortellini salad, 84
  Robert's chili, 39
  Santa Fe Cheddar soup, 60
  turkey tortellini salad, 82
  tortellini soup, 52
TORTELLINI,
  about, 53
  in...
    ricotta salad, 84
    turkey salad, 82
    tomato soup, 52
tuna, albacore, pasta salad, 92
TURKEY,
  in antipasto salad, 74
  -barley soup, 54
  -pasta mayo salad, 80
  -tortellini salad, 82
  smoked, wild rice salad, 100

Index

U

U.S. Senate bean soup, 50

V

vegetable quiche, autumn, 124
vegetarian, see MEAT-FREE.
VINAIGRETTE,
  dressing, 25
  in...
    Albacore tuna salad, 92
    antipasto pasta salad, 74
    creamy Italian dressing, 27
    fresh tomato Parmesan
      salad, 90
    garden veggie pasta
      salad, 88
    Leslie's zingy potato
      salad, 105
    Oregon shrimp pasta
      salad, 91
    Parmesan vinaigrette
      dressing, 26
    pasta a la Greek salad, 89
    pesto pasta salad, 73
    ricotta tortellini salad, 84
    spinach-chicken pasta
      salad, 76
    turkey pasta mayo
      salad, 80
    turkey tortellini salad, 82
VINEGAR,
  about, 17-19
  apple cider, 18
  Balsamic, 18
  distilled, 18
  in dressings, 17
  fruit, 19
  herb, 18
  malt, 18
  rice, 18, 103
  wine, red and white, 17
  how to make, 18-19

W

walnut oil, about, 20
wild rice, about, 103
wild rice and turkey
  salad, 100
wine vinegar, about, 17
Worcestershire, about, 30

Y

yeast, baker's, about, 138-9

Z

zest, orange and lemon,
  about, 141

Cooking at the Café
2910 N.W. Hayes
Corvallis, OR 97330
(503) 757-7663

Cooking at the Café
lunch and dinner fare

Name _____
Address _____
City _____ State _____ Zip Code _____

Please send ___ copies of "Cooking at the Café" at $14.95 per copy plus $3.25 per copy to cover shipping and handling. Make checks payable to Cooking at the Café. Thank you!

Cooking at the Café
2910 N.W. Hayes
Corvallis, OR 97330
(503) 757-7663

Cooking at the Café
lunch and dinner fare

Name _____
Address _____
City _____ State _____ Zip Code _____

Please send ___ copies of "Cooking at the Café" at $14.95 per copy plus $3.25 per copy to cover shipping and handling. Make checks payable to Cooking at the Café. Thank you!

Cooking at the Café
2910 N.W. Hayes
Corvallis, OR 97330
(503) 757-7663

Cooking at the Café
lunch and dinner fare

Name _____
Address _____
City _____ State _____ Zip Code _____

Please send ___ copies of "Cooking at the Café" at $14.95 per copy plus $3.25 per copy to cover shipping and handling. Make checks payable to Cooking at the Café. Thank you!

Having self-published "Cooking at the Café" I have become the zealous marketer of my cookbook. I'm constantly looking for additional stores to sell in. You can help by listing some favorite stores that you feel would be appropriate for my cookbook. Consider bookstores, gift shops, cooking and kitchen stores, and food co-ops. Thanks!

Store name_____
Store address_____
City_____ State_____ Zip Code_____
Store name_____
Store address_____
City_____ State_____ Zip Code_____

Having self-published "Cooking at the Café" I have become the zealous marketer of my cookbook. I'm constantly looking for additional stores to sell in. You can help by listing some favorite stores that you feel would be appropriate for my cookbook. Consider bookstores, gift shops, cooking and kitchen stores, and food co-ops. Thanks!

Store name_____
Store address_____
City_____ State_____ Zip Code_____
Store name_____
Store address_____
City_____ State_____ Zip Code_____

Having self-published "Cooking at the Café" I have become the zealous marketer of my cookbook. I'm constantly looking for additional stores to sell in. You can help by listing some favorite stores that you feel would be appropriate for my cookbook. Consider bookstores, gift shops, cooking and kitchen stores, and food co-ops. Thanks!

Store name_____
Store address_____
City_____ State_____ Zip Code_____
Store name_____
Store address_____
City_____ State_____ Zip Code_____